HINGE PICTURES

EIGHT WOMEN ARTISTS OCCUPY THE THIRD DIMENSION

HINGE PICTURES EIGHT WOMEN ARTISTS OCCUPY THE THIRD DIMENSION

Sarah Crowner

Julia Dault

Leslie Hewitt

Tomashi Jackson

Erin Shirreff

Adriana Varejão

Ulla von Brandenburg

Claudia Wieser

Edited and with an introduction by Andrea Andersson
and an essay by Alex Klein

siglio + Contemporary Arts Center, New Orleans

Catskill, New York + New Orleans, Louisiana 2019

Book design: Natalie Kraft
Cover design: Martha Ormiston
First edition. ISBN: 978-1-938221-22-4. Printed and bound in China.

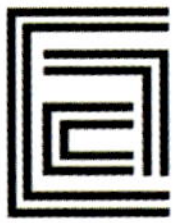

Contemporary Arts Center
900 Camp Street, New Orleans, LA 70130
www.cacno.org   t: 504.528.3805

siglio uncommon books at the intersection of art & literature

P.O. Box 111, Catskill, New York 12414
www.sigliopress.com   t: 310-857-6935   publisher@sigliopress.com

Available to the trade through D.A.P./Artbook.com
75 Broad Street, Suite 630, New York, NY 10004
t: 212-627-1999 f: 212-627-9484

Hinge Pictures: Eight Women Artists Occupy the Third Dimension runs March 14–June 16, 2019 at the Contemporary Arts Center, New Orleans.

The exhibition is curated by Andrea Andersson, PhD, The Helis Foundation Chief Curator of Visual Arts at the Contemporary Arts Center, New Orleans.

This artists' book is a collaboration between the Contemporary Arts Center, New Orleans and Siglio Press.

The exhibition is supported by The Helis Foundation, the Andy Warhol Foundation for the Visual Arts, Sydney & Walda Besthoff, and an anonymous gift.

Major support is provided by Étant donnés Contemporary Art, a program of the French American Cultural Exchange (FACE) Foundation, and the National Endowment for the Arts.

Additional funding is provided by the Visual Arts Exhibition Fund with generous contributions from the Azby Fund, Bryan Bailey, Valerie Besthoff, Anna & Scott Dunbar, Felicity Property Co., and Aimée & Mike Siegel.

This exhibition is also supported in part by a Community Arts Grant made possible by the City of New Orleans and administered by the Arts Council New Orleans, as well as by a grant from the Louisiana Division of the Arts, Office of Cultural Development, Department of Culture, Recreation and Tourism, in cooperation with the Louisiana State Arts Council.

Additional support by Marianne Boesky Gallery, New York and Aspen; Gagosian; Casey Kaplan, New York; Perrotin; Pilar Corrias Gallery, London; Sikkema Jenkins, & Co., New York; and Tilton Gallery, New York.

Andrea Andersson

Introduction: Principles of Relationship

Perhaps make
a hinge picture.
(folding yardsticks, book . . . .)
develop
the principle of the hinge
in the displacements
1st in the plane 2nd in space

. . .

perhaps introduce it
in the Pendu femelle

—Marcel Duchamp, *The Green Box*

n 1960, George Heard Hamilton published the first complete typo-graphic translation of Duchamp's *Green Box* in English. A trade edition of 1000 copies, with two subsequent reprintings of 1000 and 2500 copies respectively between 1960 and 1976, the publication was defining for both the translation and circulation of ideas from the pre-war European avant-garde to a post-war America. Garnering significant attention within the art community in New York, *The Bride Stripped Bare by Her Bachelors, Even*—described by Rosalind Krauss as "a publishing landmark for postwar art"—served as a vehicle for aesthetic philosophy,[1] but moreover as a meditation on an aesthetics of "doubts" and "doubletakes."[2]

The original *Green Box*, produced by Duchamp in 1934 (an edition of 320 copies), was a cardboard box, containing one color plate and ninety-three reproductions of notes and drawings, written between

1 See Lawrence Alloway, "The Bride Stripped Bare by Her Bachelors, Even," in *Design* 150 (1960) and Jasper Johns, "Duchamp" in *Scrap* 2 (December 23, 1960). In her 1965 essay "Jasper Johns," Rosalind Krauss describes the ways that Johns' language in his own sketchbooks took on a new character after studying Hamilton's translation: "Probably not in the spirit of self-conscious imitation but certainly as some kind of referential action, Johns' notes to himself in his own sketchbooks took on more and more of the ring of Duchamp's enigmatic prescriptions for *The Large Glass.*" See Rosalind Krauss, "Jasper Johns," *The Lugano Review*, Vol. 1/2 (1965).

2 In his postscript, Hamilton writes of Duchamp's 1934 edition of the *Green Box*: "What the facsimiles present, above all else, is the evidence of a prolonged meditation on art—a conscious probing of the limits of aesthetic creation. They convey the doubts, the rethinks and doubletakes, the flat bewilderment and the moments of assurance; the pauses and reaffirmations are there, the winces, private sniggers and nervous ticks." See Marcel Duchamp, *The Bride Stripped Bare by Her Bachelors, Even*, a typographic version by Richard Hamilton of Marcel Duchamp's Green Box (London and Bradford: Percy Lund, Humphries and Co. Ltd, 1960), n.p.

Perhaps make
a <u>hinge</u>
<u>picture.</u>
(folding yardstick, book . . . .)
develop
the <u>principle of the hinge</u>
in the displacements
1st in the plane 2nd in space

find an <u>automatic description</u>
<u>of the hinge</u>

———————————————

    perhaps introduce it
    in the Pendu femelle

1911 and 1923, to accompany, explain, and extend his great work, *La Mariée mise à nu par ses célibataires, méme,* (in translation, "The Bride Stripped Bare by Her Bachelors, Even" and more commonly referred to as *The Large Glass*). *The Large Glass* is a mixed media work, in the Arensberg Collection of the Philadelphia Museum of Art. A production in oil paint, lead foil, wire, and dust suspended between two panes of glass, it is narrated as a mechanical display of erotic desire between Duchamp's "Bride" in the upper panel and the nine "Bachelors" below. To say that the work is allegorical suggests something of its conceptual ambitions that exceed, certainly by some measures, its "pictorial expression."[3] As Hamilton lamented in his appendix notes, the "danger of [Duchamp's] position, its utter and daring originality, as well as his uncompromising and self-adjusting truth, lies in the fact that after almost fifty years the 'Bride' is still not a picture for most people."[4]

It is not a picture in the way that Duchamp's *Bicycle Wheel* (1913), *Bottle Rack* (1914), or *Fountain* (1917) figure in the collective imagination or in the cultural debates over what functions as art in the twentieth and twenty-first centuries. And as not a picture for most people, the work serves as an unlikely foundation for an exhibition about the legacy of modernism in the work of eight contemporary international women artists. But if not a picture (and as a masterwork by the father of non-retinal art, we can concede and rest this point), then we can approach *The Large Glass* as a philosophy or a system of logic—for as Duchamp himself wrote, "the ideas in the glass are more important than the actual visual realizations."

Hinge Pictures: Eight Women Artists Occupy the Third Dimension is an exhibition about an idea that is an event—an idea to pivot—to move between positions in space and in history. It is an idea that refuses the fixity perhaps mockingly suggested between Duchamp's two plates of glass (a still life with wire, a freeze frame of dust) and signals toward multiple perspectives. Like *The Large Glass*, it operates by necessity both in the gallery and on the page—in place and in distribution. It opens and closes. But a hinge is also bound to its point of connection, point of origin.

3 Ibid.
4 Ibid.

Opposite: Excerpt from *The Bride Stripped Bare by Her Bachelors, Even.* Further excerpts precede each artist's section.

On the enormity of Duchamp's undertaking, Hamilton explains that "[the artist] had to call in question all traditional values, all systems of aesthetics, the whole history of art." The artist's ambivalence, his doubt is made visible in his original notes and the subsequent facsimiles in the form of "torn edges, blots, erasures and occasional illegibility." Hamilton describes Duchamp as a prophet of Heisenberg's principle of uncertainty. A theory in quantum physics regarding the relationship between momentum and position, the uncertainty principle speaks to conditions of knowledge and might be applied more expansively as the more we know, the more we know that we don't know.

In these pages, artists Ulla von Brandenburg, Sarah Crowner, Julia Dault, Leslie Hewitt, Tomashi Jackson, Erin Shirreff, Adriana Varejão, and Claudia Wieser establish a palimpsestual relationship with Duchamp's writings and the history of modernism by extension. The book is comprised of eight successive artists' signatures, just as the exhibition is comprised of eight successive artists' galleries. Each signature in the book begins with a sheet of vellum, treated and marked by the artist, and overlayed on top of a page selected from Duchamp's 1960 publication. The book and the exhibition afford responses and challenges to an invitation by Duchamp "to make a hinge picture," to depart from the flat plane of the wall in the occupation of three-dimensional space.

The eight artists in this book and in the exhibition apply the principle of the hinge and the principle of uncertainty in practices that question the forms they inherit and their instrinsic politics. As such, they interrogate the very logic of Duchamp's *objets trouvés* and locate the significance of the readymade in its capacity to be repositioned. *Hinge Pictures: Eight Women Artists Occupy the Third Dimension* is a demonstration of a confrontation with the patrimony of European modernism and a feminist formalism defined by principles of relation-ship across time and space.

Erin Shirreff

Kind of Sub-Title

Delay in Glass

Use "delay" instead of "picture" or
"painting"; "picture on glass" becomes
"delay in glass"—but "delay in
glass" does not mean "picture
on glass"—

It's merely a way
of succeeding in no longer thinking
that the thing in question is
a picture—to make a "delay" of it
in the most general way possible,
not so much in the different meanings
in which "delay" can be taken, but
rather in their indecisive reunion
"delay"—a "delay in glass"

as you would say a "poem in prose"

or a spittoon in silver

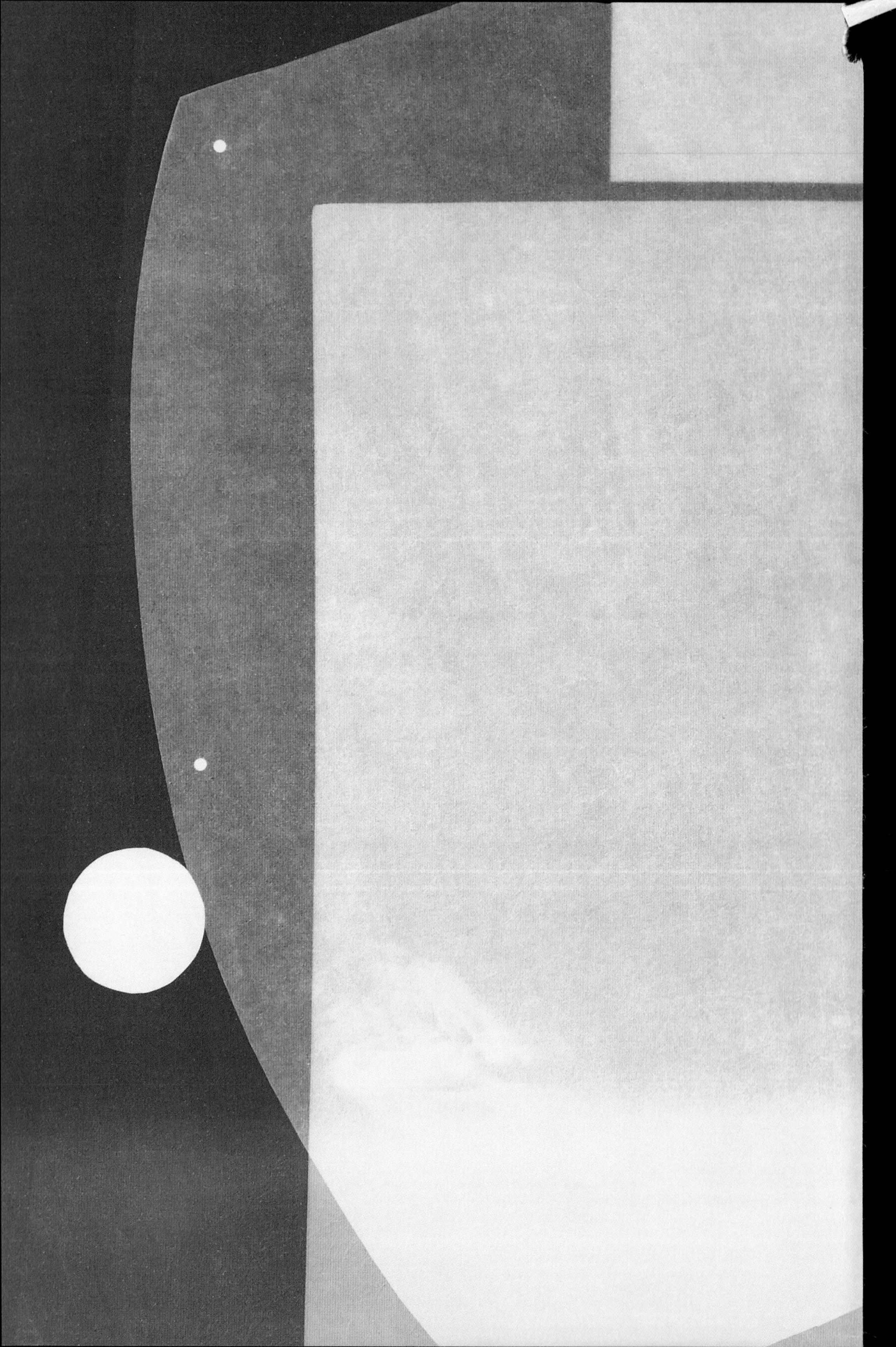

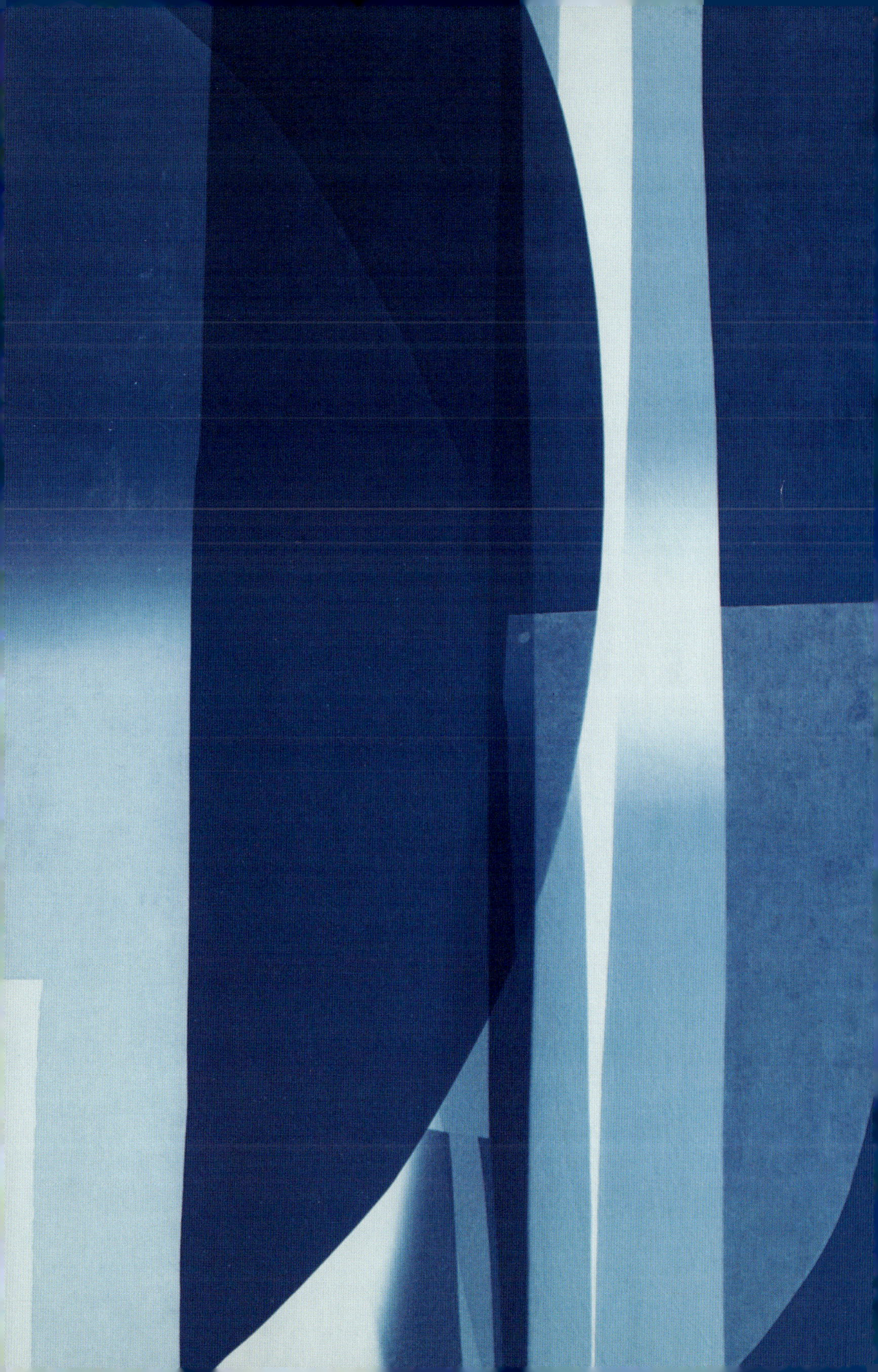

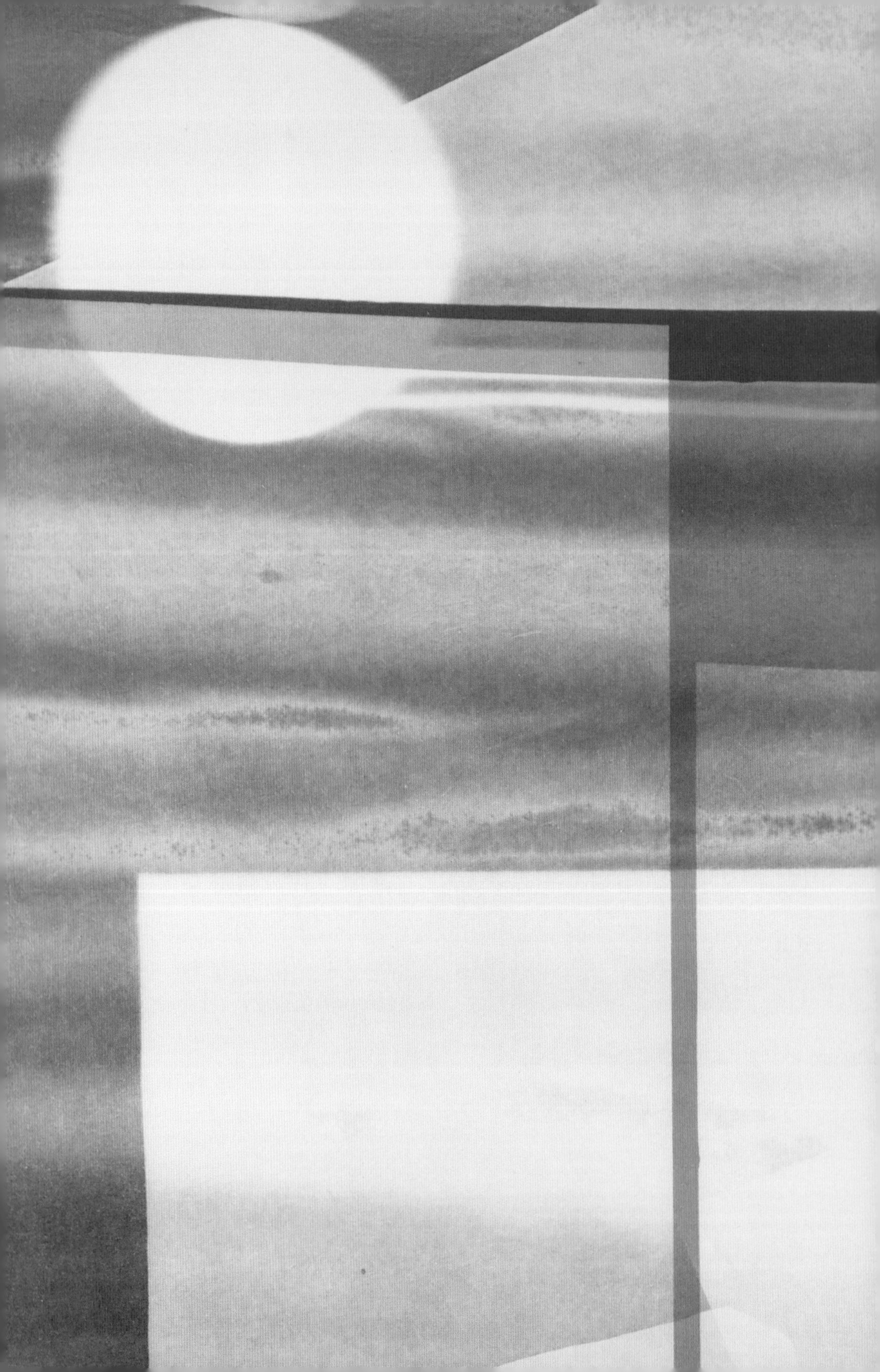

ERIN SHIRREFF's (b. 1975, Kelowna, Canada) diverse body of work, including photography, video, and sculpture, is united by her interest in the ways we experience three-dimensional forms in an age in which our perception is almost invariably mediated by still and moving images. Her work explores the gap between objects and their representations, and the materials (and materiality) of image-making. As amalgams of analog and digital materials and processes, Shirreff's work presents as an investigation of scale, translations, and possible relationships between picture and form. The passage of time and the effects of natural and artificial light are ideas and motifs that recur in Shirreff's work and are forces intrinsic to the process of making cyanotype photographs, a recurring subject of investigation for the artist.

Leslie Hewitt

"What I call the "invention" of the origins aims to identify, within a broad-
er historical perspective that studies the representation of architecture in
photography, the time when the relationship between photography and architecture was constituted as a territory of
sharing principles or modes of relating to the built
environment, rather than a representational relationship of submissive order (photography
serving the registry of architecture)."

"What I call the "invention" of the origins aims to identify, within a broad-
er historical perspective that studies the representation of architecture in
photography, the time when the relationship between photography and architecture was constituted as a territory of
sharing principles or modes of relating to the built
environment, rather than a representational relationship of submissive order (photography
serving the registry of architecture)."

Excerpt from GAZING ARCHITECTURE, ARCHITECTURES OF THE GAZE. PHOTOGRAPHIC IMAGINATION OF THE BUILT SPACE by JUNNA CAMBRAIA MORTIMER (2015)

Preface

Given 1. the waterfall

   2. the illuminating gas,

one will determine
we shall determine the conditions

for the instantaneous State of Rest (or allegorical appearance)

of a succession [of a group] of various facts

seeming to necessitate each other

under certain laws, in order to isolate the sign
   the
of accordance between, on the one hand,
   all the   (?)
this State of Rest (capable of innumerable eccentricities)

and, on the other, a choice of Possibilities

authorized by these laws and also

determining them.

For the instantaneous state of rest = bring in

the term: extra-rapid

We shall determine the conditions of [the] best

exposé of the extra-rapid State of Rest [of the

extra-rapid exposure (= allegorical appearance).

of a group . . . . . . etc.

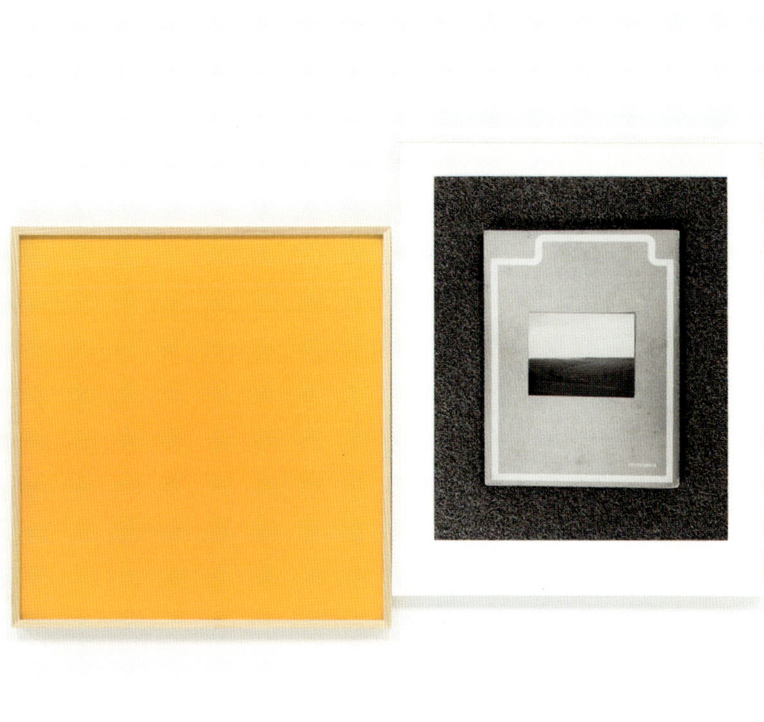

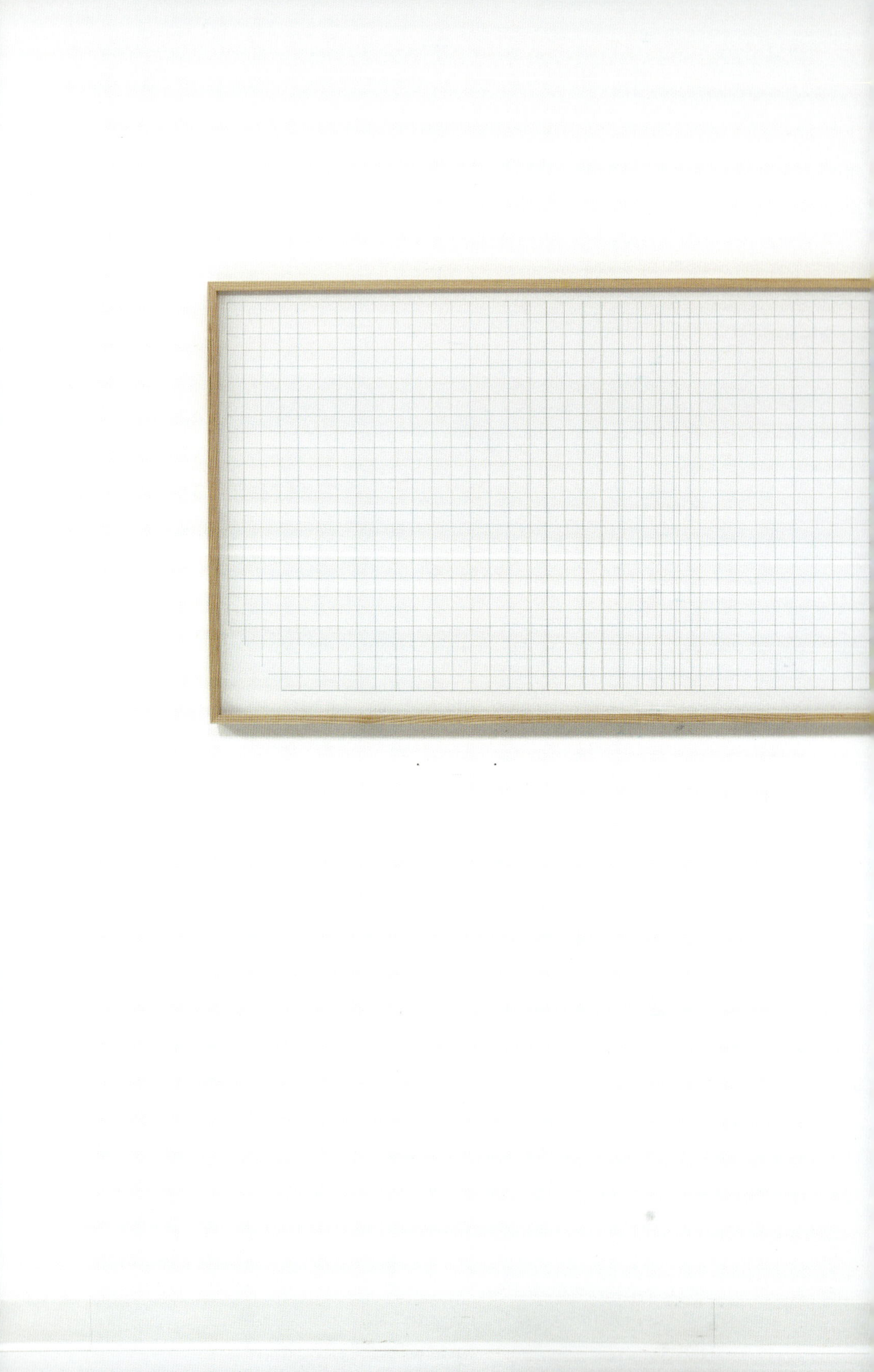

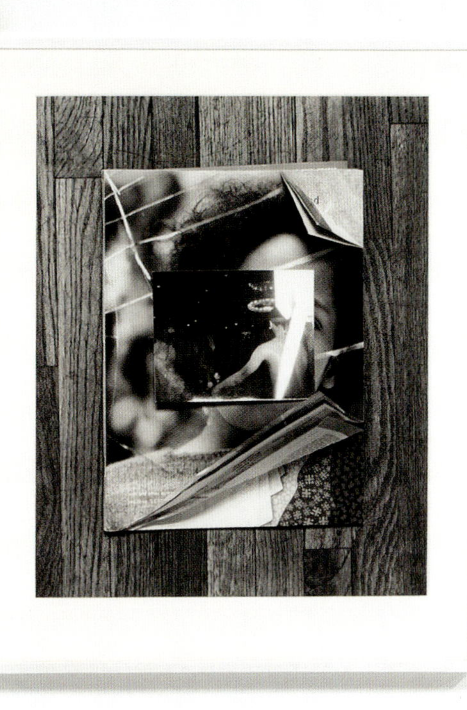

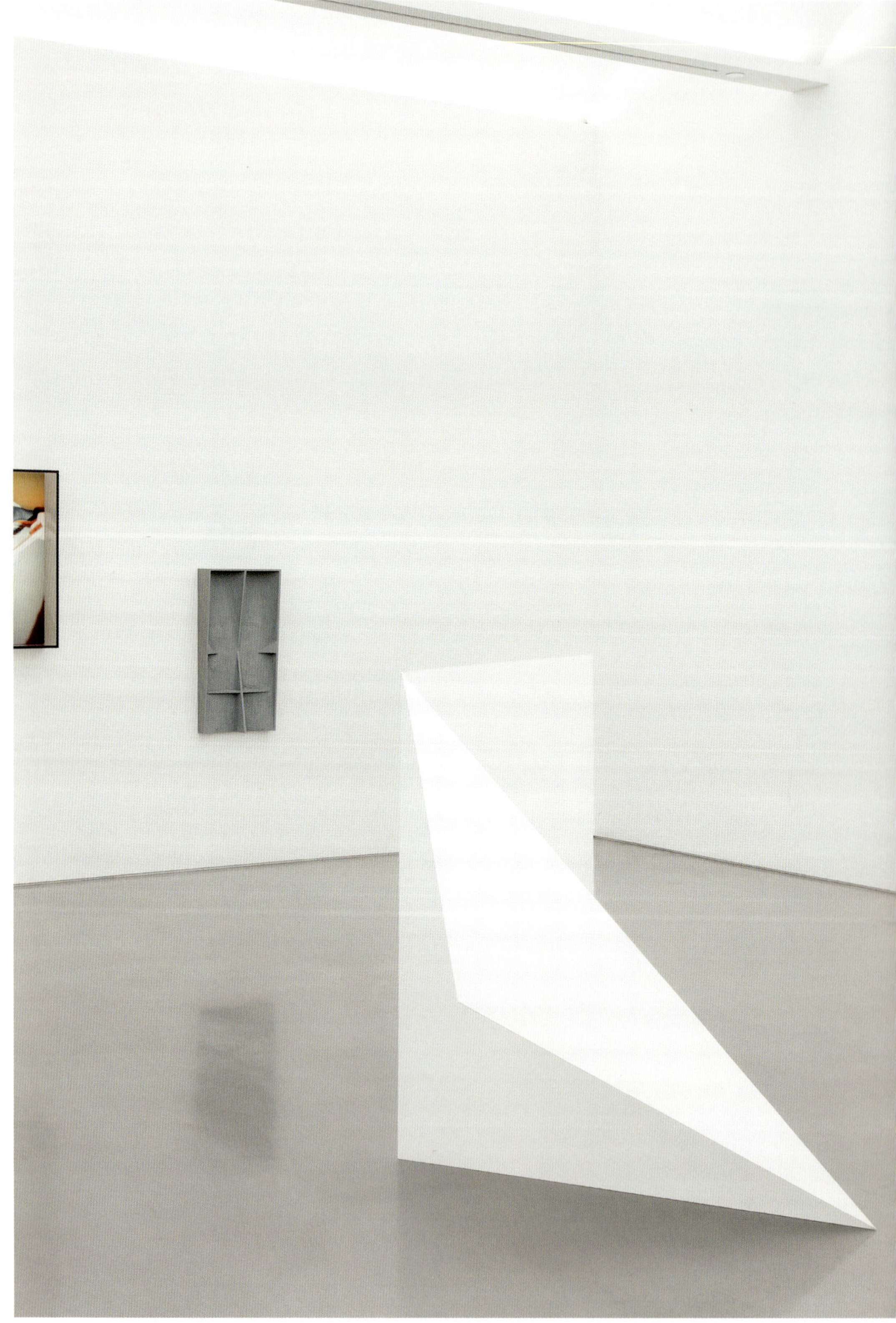

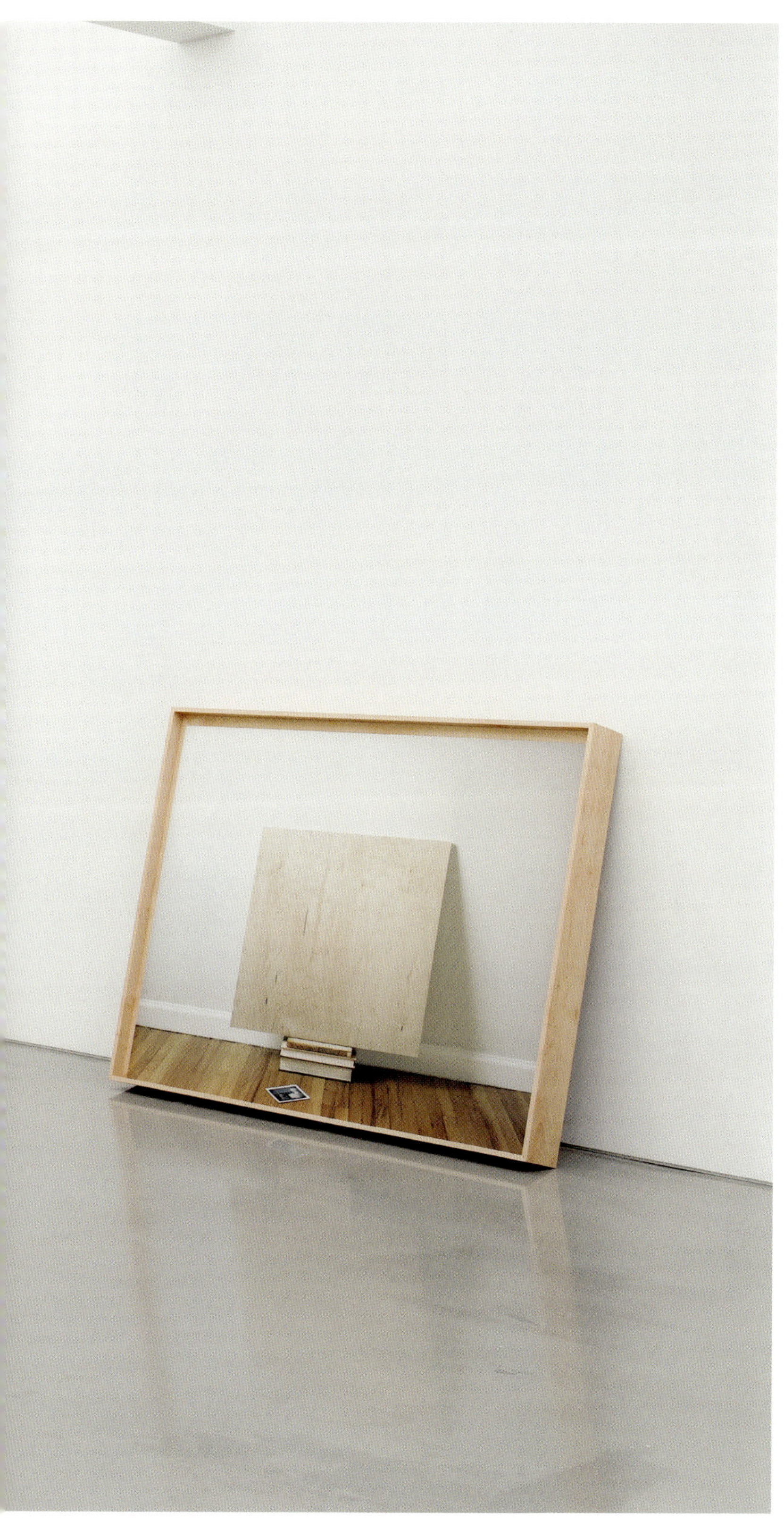

LESLIE HEWITT (b. 1977, New York, United States) lives and works in New York. Working with photography, sculpture, and site-specific installations, Hewitt addresses fluid notions of time. Her photographed still life compositions—comprised of political, social, and personal materials—result in multiple histories embedded in sculptural, architectural, and abstract forms. Mundane objects and structures open into complex systems of knowledge. This perceptual slippage is what attracts Hewitt to both the illusions of film (still and moving photography) and the undeniable presence of physical objects (sculptures). Exploring this as an artist rather than as a historiographer, Hewitt draws parallels between the formal appearance of things and their significance to a collective sense of history and political consciousness in contemporary art and everyday life.

Ulla von Brandenburg

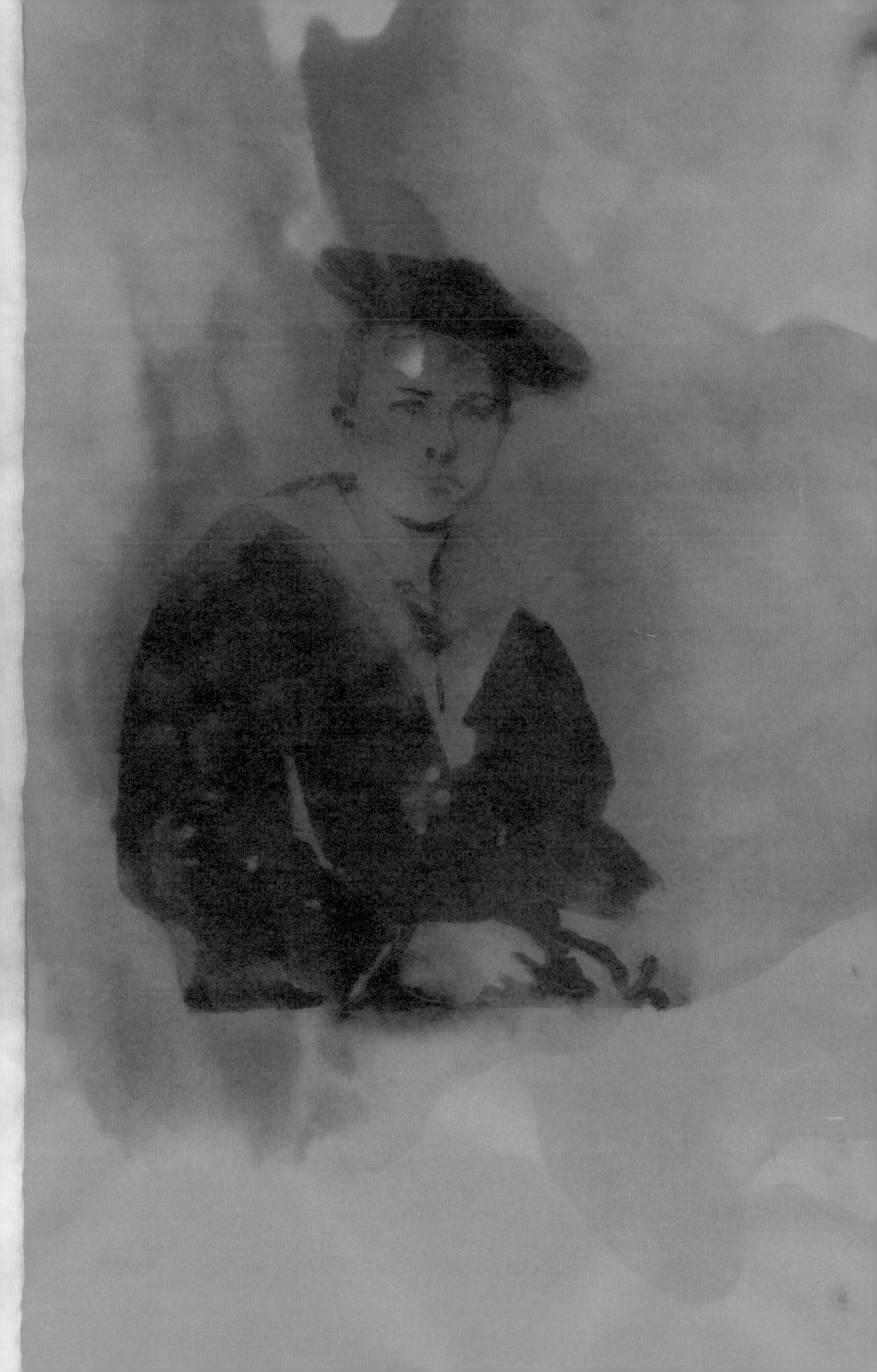

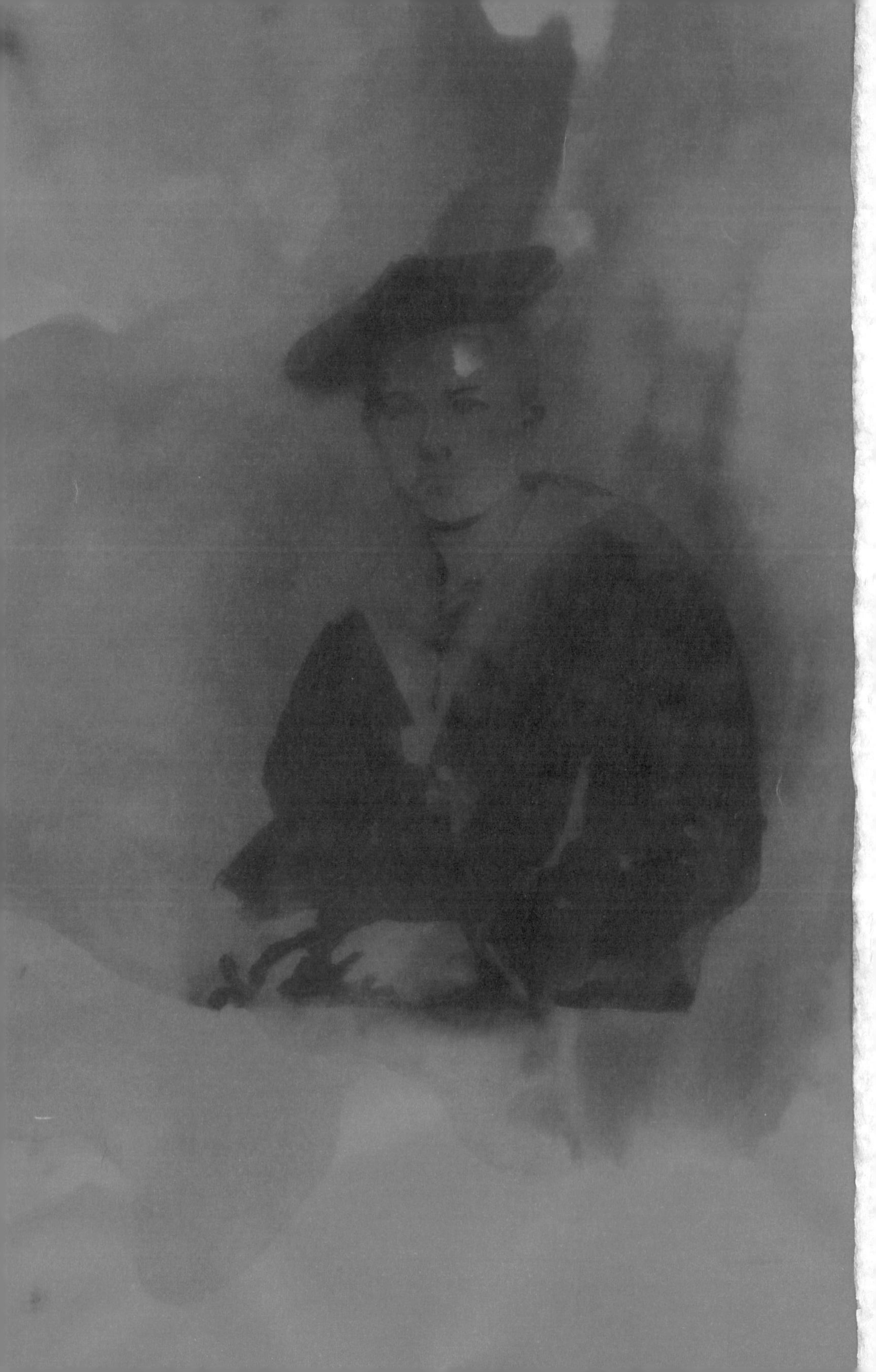

The Pendu femelle
  is the form
  in <u>ordinary perspective</u>
of a Pendu femelle
for which one could perhaps
try to discover
the true form

———————

This comes from the
fact that any
form is the perspective
of another form
according to a certain <u>vanishing point</u>
and a certain <u>distance</u>

Isabelle Wilhelmine Marie Eberhardt (1877-1904) was a Swiss writer, journalist, and war reporter.

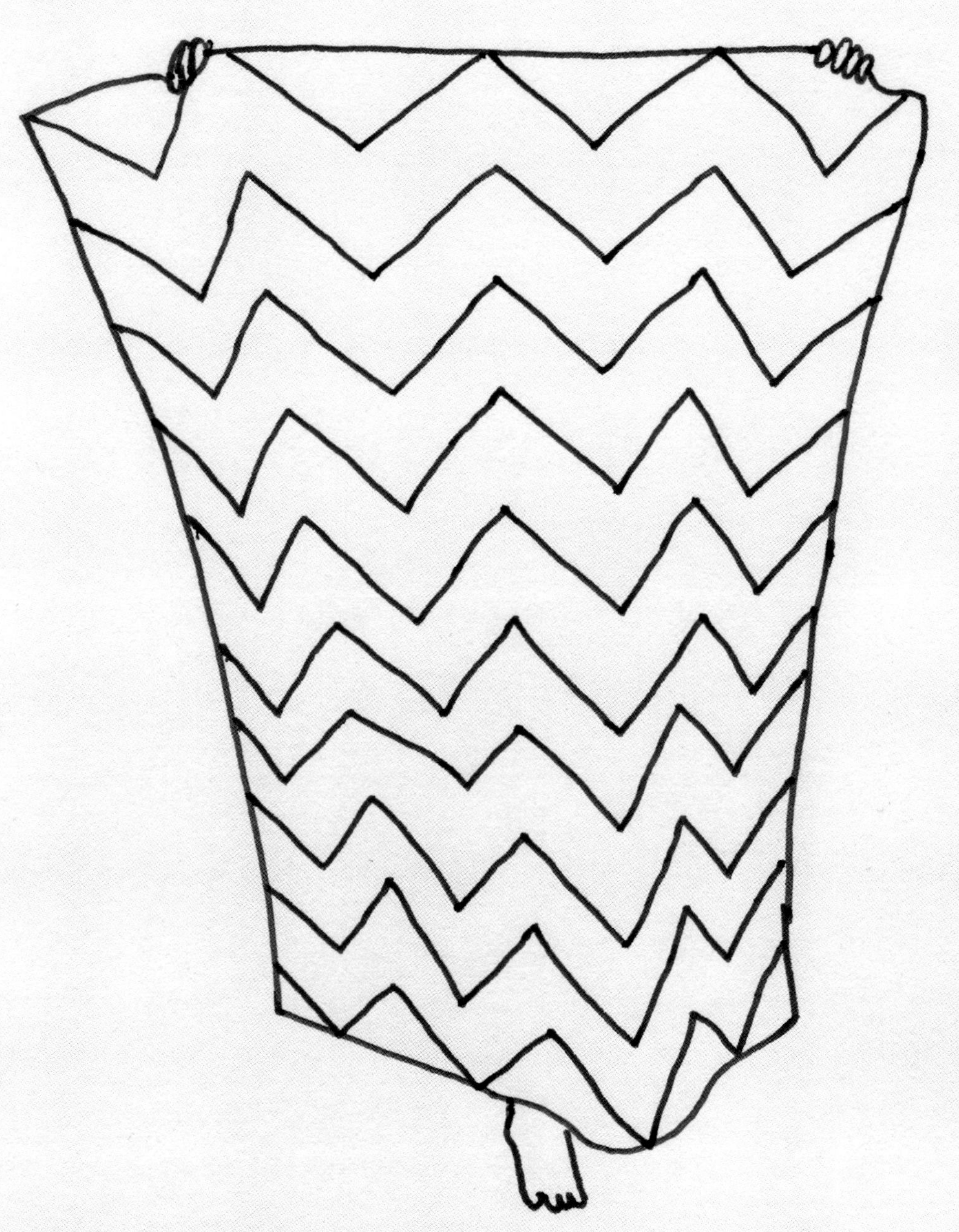

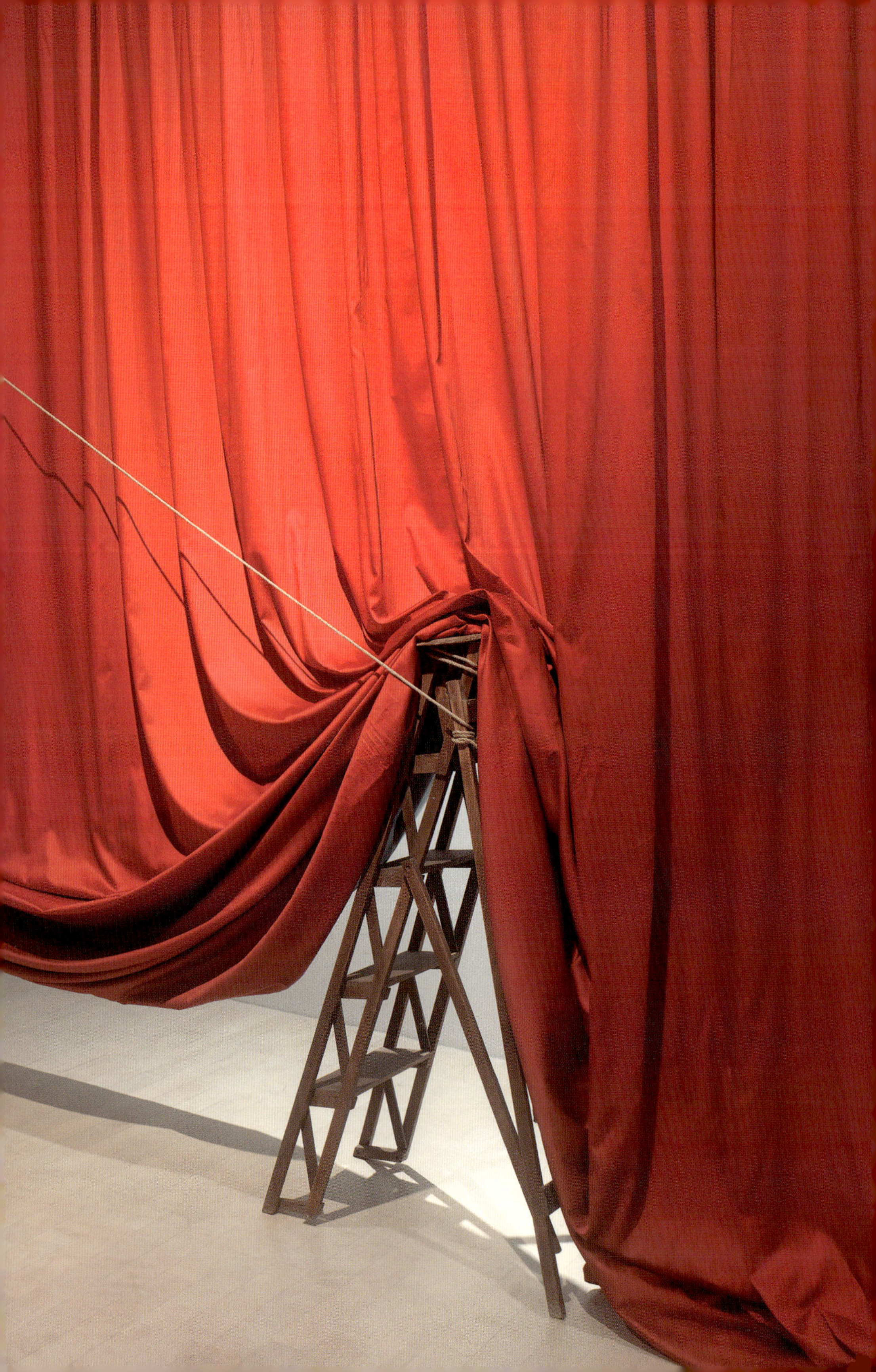

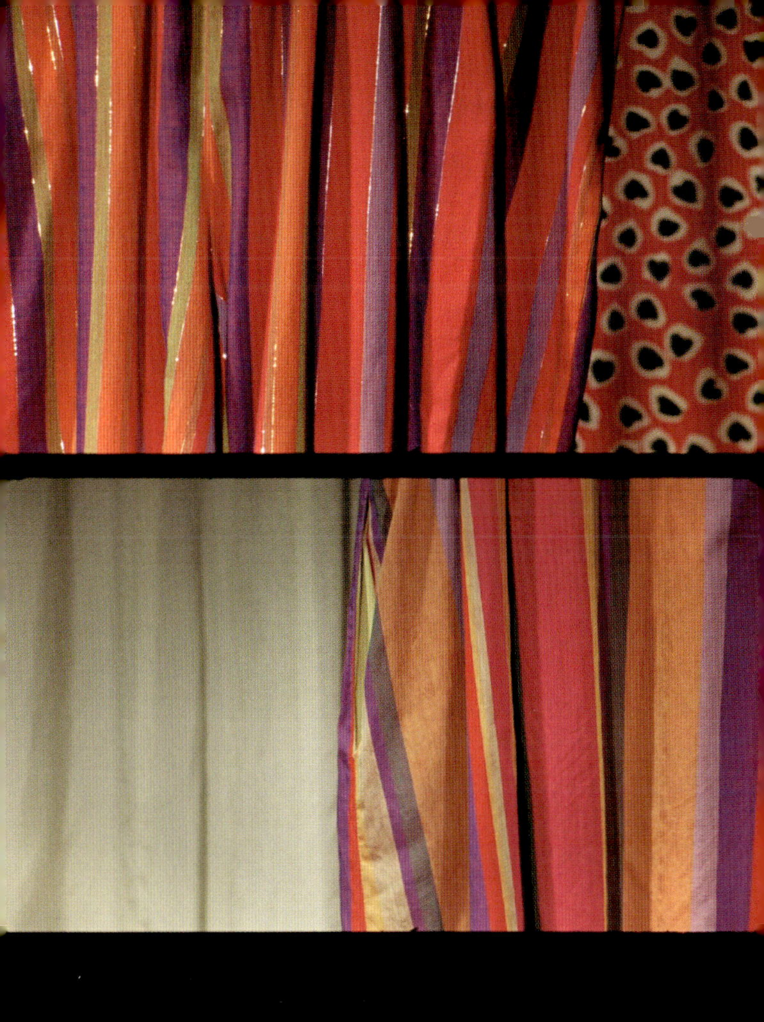

Like women before and after her, she employed male attributes
to make her place in a world dominated by men.

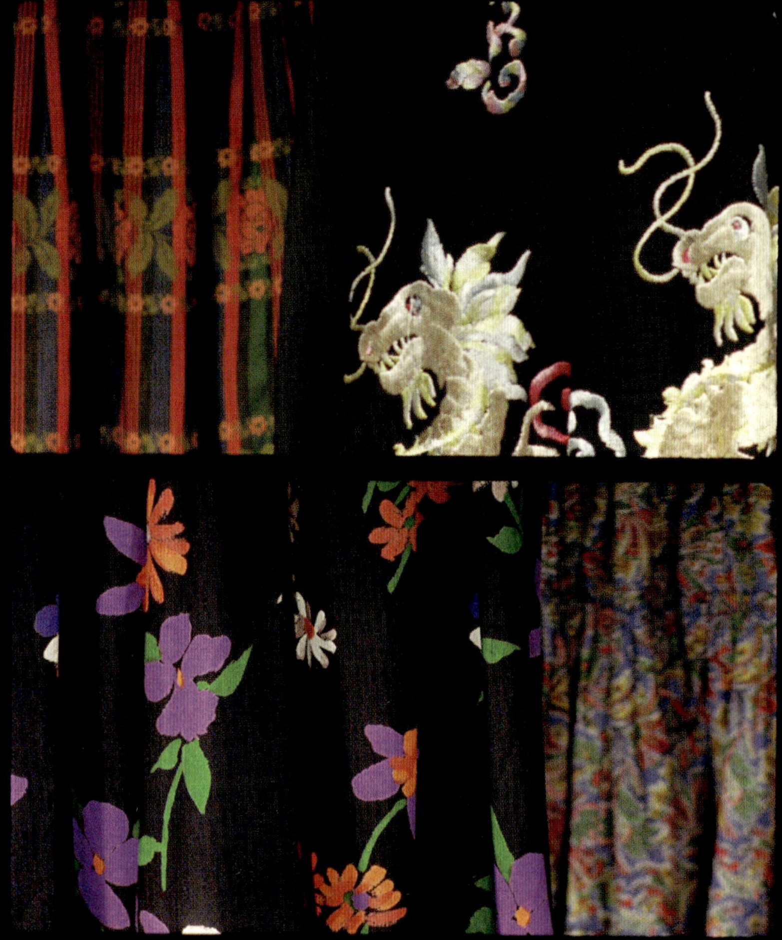

Using different male pseudonyms, such as Mahmoud Saasi or Nicolas Podolinsky, she published a series of novels, travel stories, and political writings advocating anti-colonial ideas.

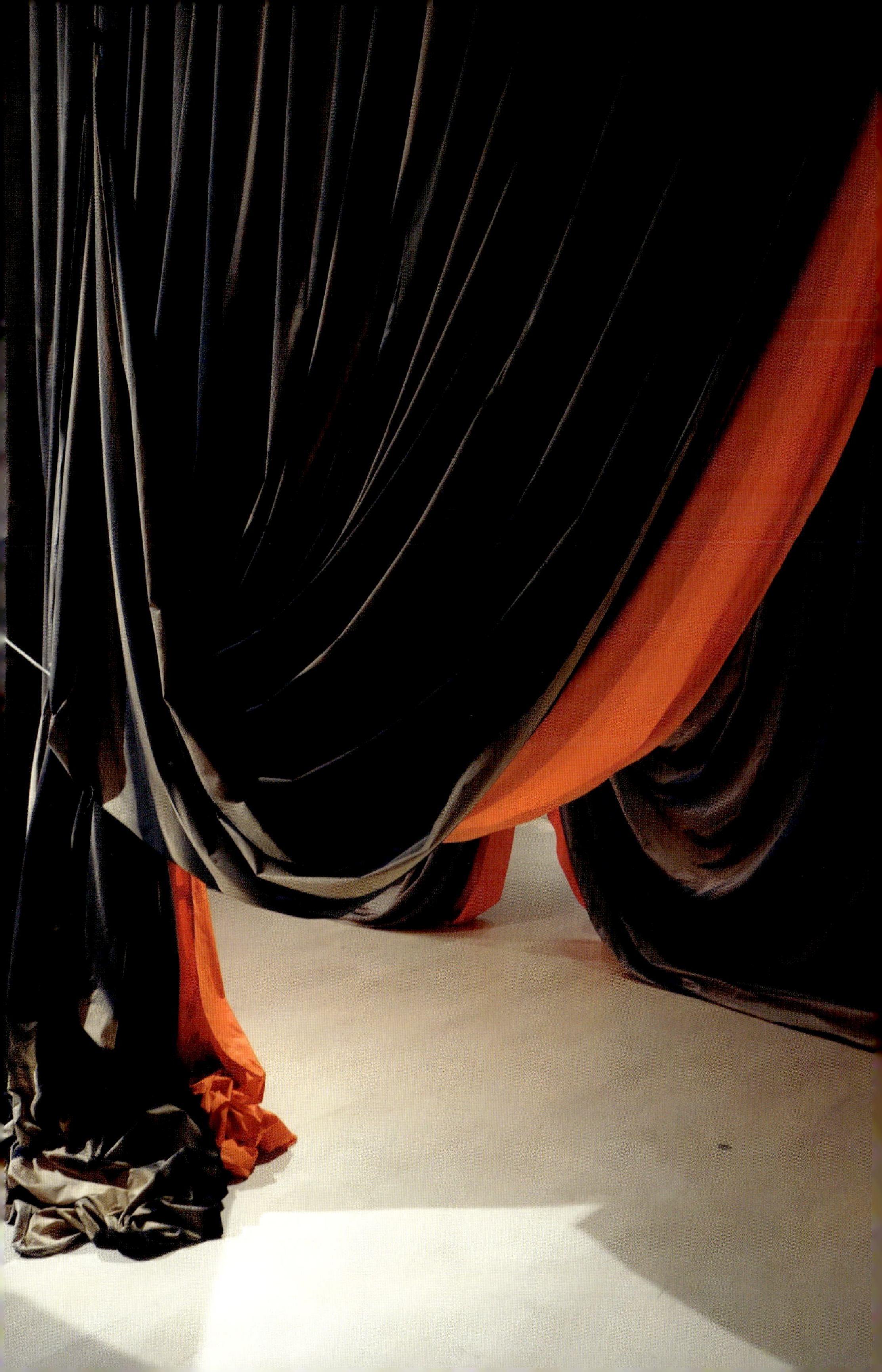

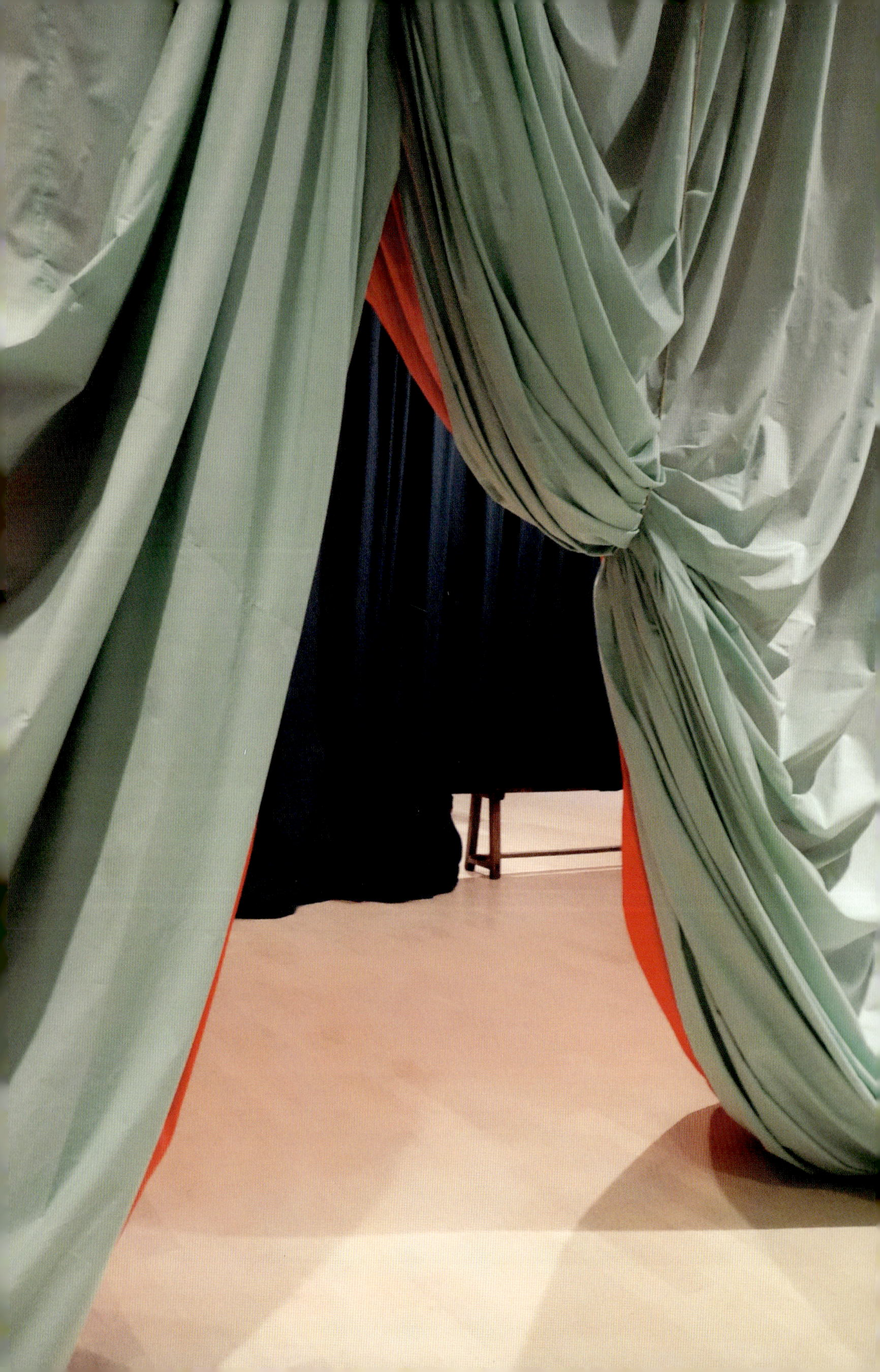

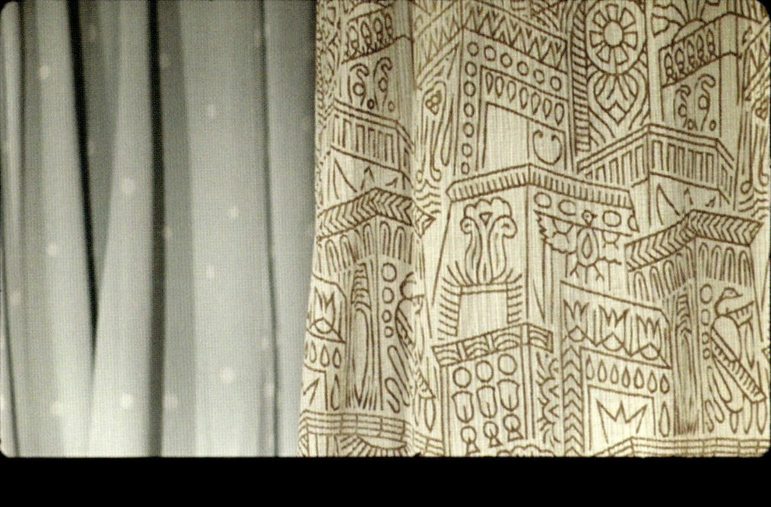

Passionate about North Africa and Islam (to which she converted), Isabelle Eberhardt travelled all around Maghreb and Sahara Desert to pursue her research, dressed up like a man.

ULLA VON BRANDENBURG's (b. 1974, Karlsruhe, Germany) practice builds through films, performances, installations, objects, music, paintings and drawings. With great interest in popular ceremonies and social ritual, Brandenburg creates images which gradually distance themselves from reality and shift our expectations. Her practice draws from her research of abstraction, collage, colorimetry, psychoanalysis, bodily and costume patterns, and human gesture. Her immersive and labyrinthine installations made of fabric, her upside-down architectures, and her workable wooden structures are designed as watching apparatuses for her films. Ulla von Brandenburg considers the viewer as an actor in the work, someone who takes part in its creation.

Adriana Varejão

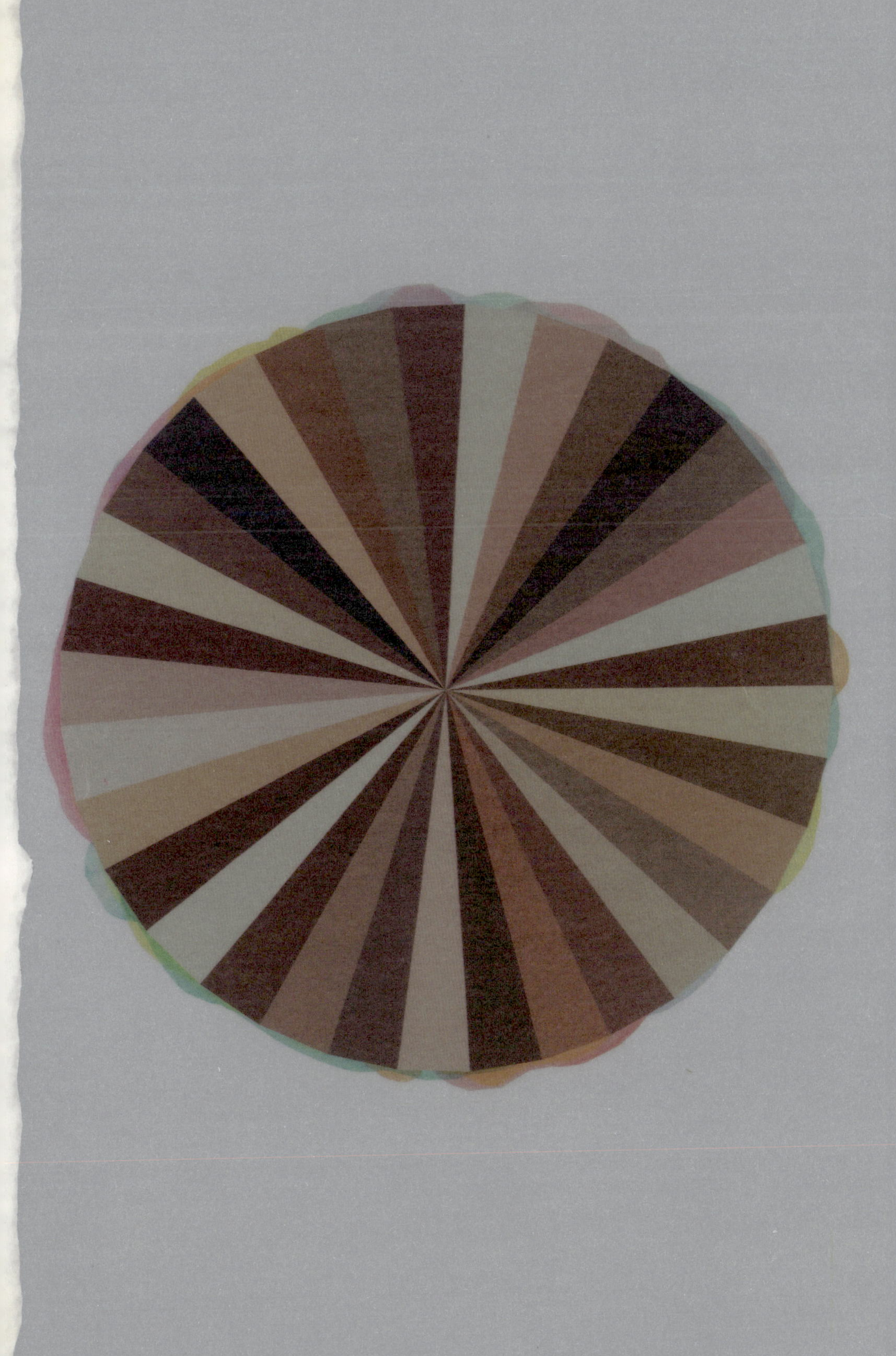

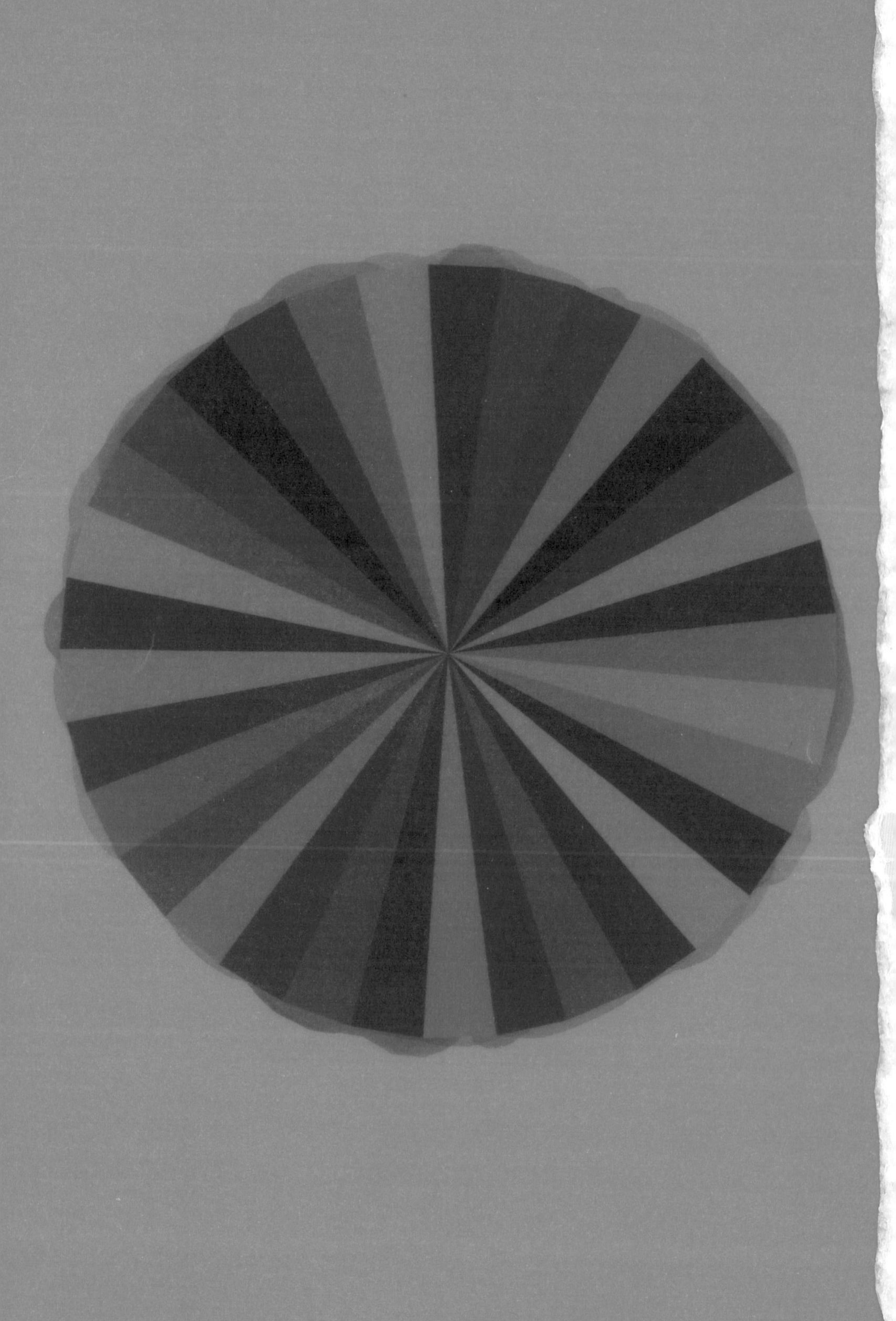

Breeding of Colors

— In the greenhouse
  [On a glass plate, colors seen
  transparently].

   Mixture of flowers of color i.e.

each color still in its optical state:

Perfumes $^{(?)}$of reds, of

blues of greens or of grays heightened

towards yellow blue red

or of weaker maroons. (the

whole in scales.). These perfumes

with physiological rebound can

be neglected and extracted in

an imprisonment for the fruit.

   Only, the fruit still has to

avoid being eaten. It's this

dryness of "nuts and raisins,, that you

get in the ripe imputrescent

colors. (rarefied colors.).

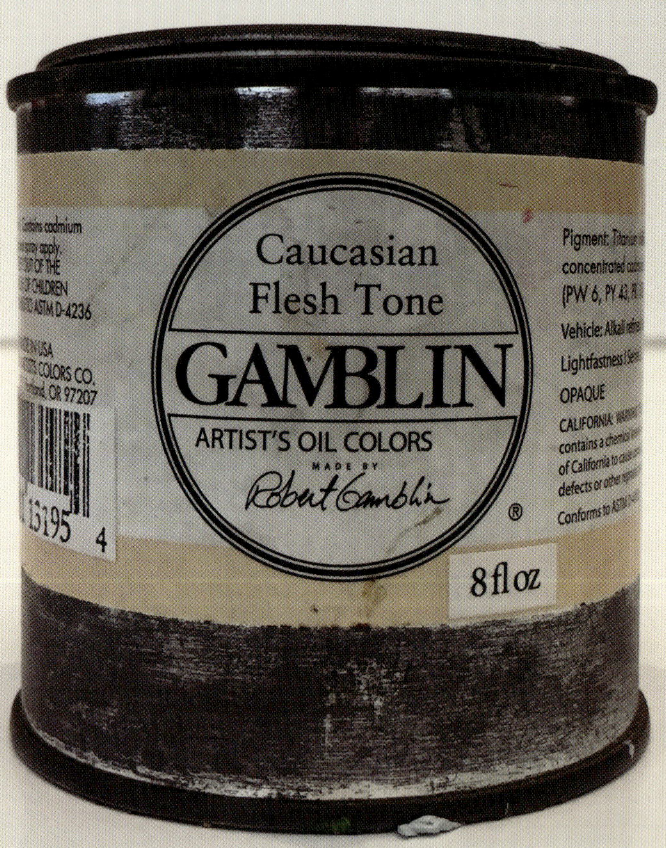
contains cadmium
apply.
OUT OF THE
CHILDREN
ASTM D-4236
IN USA
COLORS CO.
OR 97207
15195 4
Caucasian
Flesh Tone
GAMBLIN
ARTIST'S OIL COLORS
MADE BY
Robert Gamblin
8 fl oz
Pigment: Titanium
concentrated cad
(PW 6, PY 43, P
Vehicle: Alkali refin
Lightfastness I Ser
OPAQUE
CALIFORNIA: WARNING
contains a chemical
of California to cause
defects or other
Conforms to ASTM

Polvo

If every discourse on race justifies itself with the
need for scientific classification, it is in the
precise act of naming that cultures have made racial
differences a meaningful and relevant aspect of
social life. Meanings are not inherent to things or
events. Anthropology has demonstrated that there are
still tribes, such as the Indonesian Dani, who do not
name colors, except as "dark" or "light." Naming skin
color is not a neutral act, but a cultural construct
with deep social consequences. In Portugues, "polvo"
means "octopus" and sounds like "povo," the word for
"people." Curiously, octopus ink contains melanin,
the pigment responsible for the colour of human skin.

1 acastanhada	33 bugrezinha-escura	65 galegada	97 morena-roxa
2 agalegada	34 burro-quando-foge	66 jambo	98 morena-ruiva
3 alva	35 cabocla	67 laranja	99 morena-trigueira
4 alva escura	36 cabo-verde	68 lilás	100 moreninha
5 alvarenta	37 café	69 loira	101 mulata
6 alvarinta	38 café-com-leite	70 loira-clara	102 mulatinha
7 alva rosada	39 canela	71 loura	103 negra
8 alvinha	40 canelada	72 lourinha	104 negrota
9 amarela	41 cardão	73 malaia	105 pálida
10 amarelada	42 castanha	74 marinheira	106 paraíba
11 amarela-queimada	43 castanha-clara	75 marrom	107 parda
12 amarelosa	44 castanha-escura	76 meio-amarela	108 parda-clara
13 amorenada	45 chocolate	77 meio-branca	109 parda-morena
14 avermelhada	46 clara	78 meio-morena	110 parda-preta
15 azul	47 clarinha	79 meio-preta	111 polaca
16 azul-marinho	48 cobre	80 melada	112 pouco-clara
17 baiano	49 corada	81 mestiça	113 ouco-morena
18 bem branca	50 cor-de-café	82 miscigenação	114 pretinha
19 bem clara	51 cor-de-canela	83 mista	115 puxa-para-branco
20 bem morena	52 cor-de-cuia	84 morena	116 quase-negra
21 branca	53 cor-de-leite	85 morena-bem-chegada	117 queimada
22 branca-avermelhada	54 cor-de-ouro	86 morena-bronzeada	118 queimada-de-praia
23 branca-melada	55 cor-de-rosa	87 morena-canelada	119 queimada-de-sol
24 branca-morena	56 cor-firme	88 morena-castanha	120 regular
25 branca-pálida	57 crioula	89 morena-clara	121 retinta
26 branca-queimada	58 encerada	90 morena-cor-de-canela	122 rosa
27 branca-sardenta	59 enxofrada	91 morena-jambo	123 rosada
28 branca-suja	60 esbranquecimento	92 morenada	124 rosa-queimada
29 branquiça	61 escura	93 morena-escura	125 roxa
30 branquinha	62 escurinha	94 morena-fechada	
31 bronze	63 fogoió	95 morenão	
32 bronzeada	64 galega	93 morena-parda	

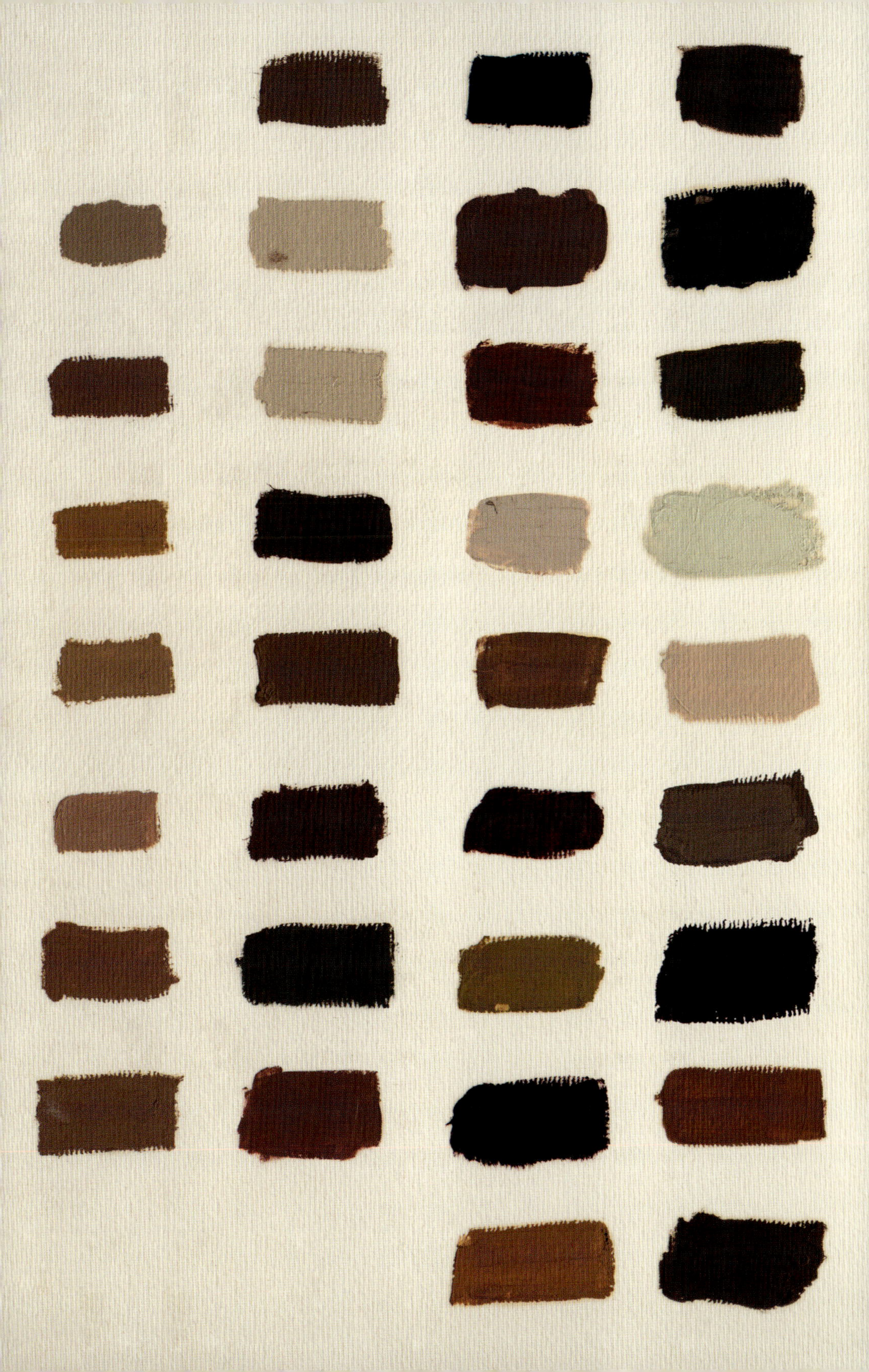

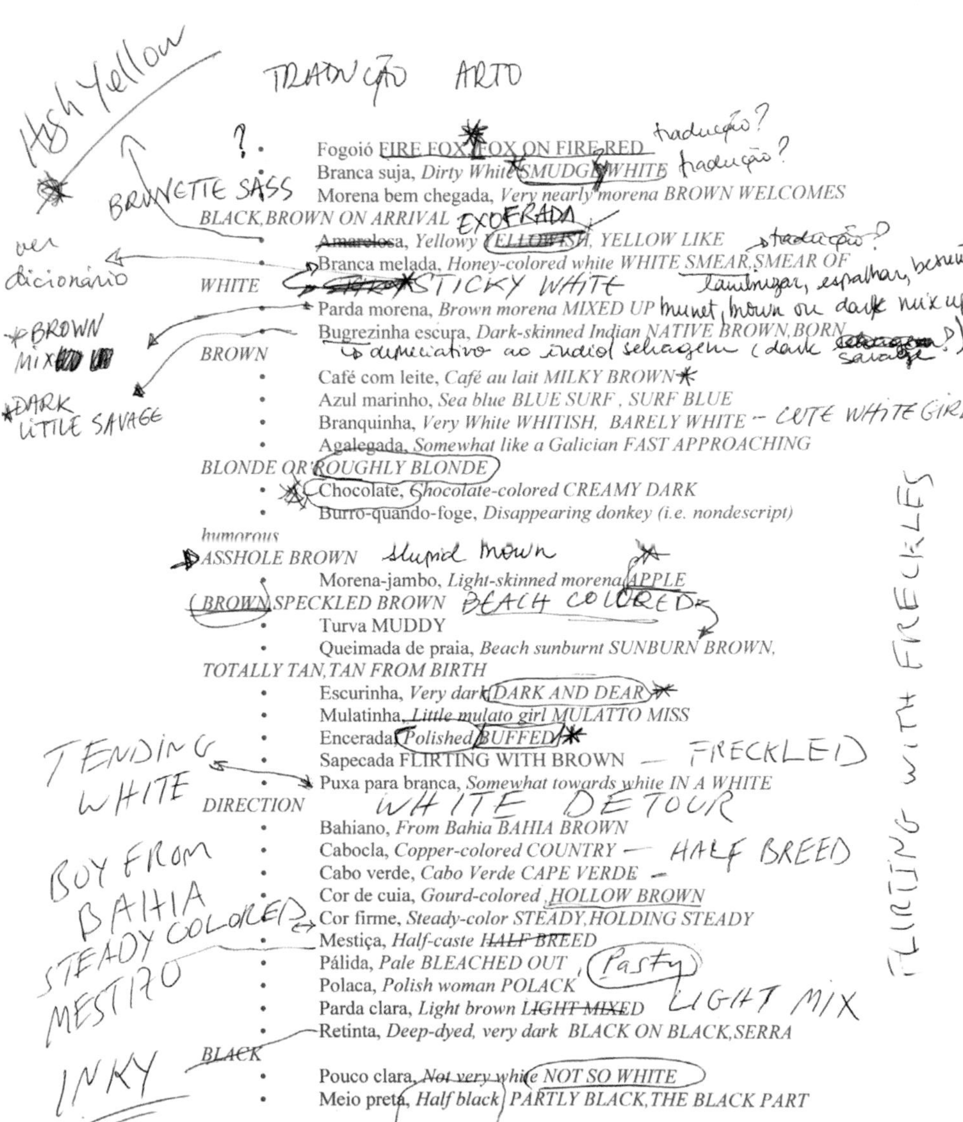

Fogoió FIRE FOX, FOX ON FIRE, RED
Branca suja, *Dirty White* SMUDGE WHITE
Morena bem chegada, *Very nearly morena* BROWN WELCOMES BLACK, BROWN ON ARRIVAL EXOFRADA
Amarelosa, *Yellowy* YELLOWISH, YELLOW LIKE
Branca melada, *Honey-colored white* WHITE SMEAR, SMEAR OF STICKY WHITE
Parda morena, *Brown morena* MIXED UP
Bugrezinha escura, *Dark-skinned Indian* NATIVE BROWN, BORN
Café com leite, *Café au lait* MILKY BROWN
Azul marinho, *Sea blue* BLUE SURF, SURF BLUE
Branquinha, *Very White* WHITISH, BARELY WHITE
Agalegada, *Somewhat like a Galician* FAST APPROACHING
Chocolate, *Chocolate-colored* CREAMY DARK
Burro-quando-foge, *Disappearing donkey (i.e. nondescript)*
Morena-jambo, *Light-skinned morena* APPLE
Turva MUDDY
Queimada de praia, *Beach sunburnt* SUNBURN BROWN,
Escurinha, *Very dark* DARK AND DEAR
Mulatinha, *Little mulato girl* MULATTO MISS
Encerada, *Polished* BUFFED
Sapecada FLIRTING WITH BROWN
Puxa para branca, *Somewhat towards white* IN A WHITE
Bahiano, *From Bahia* BAHIA BROWN
Cabocla, *Copper-colored* COUNTRY
Cabo verde, *Cabo Verde* CAPE VERDE
Cor de cuia, *Gourd-colored* HOLLOW BROWN
Cor firme, *Steady-color* STEADY, HOLDING STEADY
Mestiça, *Half-caste* HALF BREED
Pálida, *Pale* BLEACHED OUT
Polaca, *Polish woman* POLACK
Parda clara, *Light brown* LIGHT MIXED
Retinta, *Deep-dyed, very dark* BLACK ON BLACK, SERRA
Pouco clara, *Not very white* NOT SO WHITE
Meio preta, *Half black* PARTLY BLACK, THE BLACK PART

→ Brown welcomes Black   chestnut ~~brunette~~

1- FOGOIÓ - Fox on Fire Red ✓
2- BRANCA SUJA - Smudgy White ✓   sun kissed (brown)
* 3- MORENA BEM CHEGADA - Brunette Sass   ~~Sassy brunette~~
4- AMARELOSA - High Yellow ✓   Sassy Brown
5- BRANCA MELADA - Sticky White - Honey White
6- PARDA MORENA - (A Brown Mix) (segundo o Arto, o artigo
A faz toda a diferença poética) - Hybrid Brown
7- BUGRESINHA ESCURA - Born Brown (não gostamos de
Dark Little Savage afinal - parece Disney) → NATIVE BROWN
* 8- CAFE COM LEITE - Milky Brown *Milky coffee
* 9- AZUL MARINHO - Dark Blue - Blue Black.
* 10- BRANQUINHA - Cute White Girl → Snow White
* 11- AGALEGADA - Roughly Blonde → Galician ~~Fair~~ Fair
12- CHOCOLATE - Chocolat
13- BURRO-QUANDO-FOGE - Runaway Donkey
* 14- MORENA-JAMBO - Apple Brown → Fruity Brown.
15- TURVA - Muddy   Sol   Sun kissed -
* 16- QUEIMADA DE ~~PRAIA~~ - Beach Burnt (resolvemos voltar a
tradução literal de Queimada = Burnt - achamos que ficou
muito cool) ✓
→ 17- ESCURINHA - Dark and Dear + Cute Dark
18- MULATINHA - Mulatto Miss ✓   Sweet mulatto -
19- ENCERADA - Buffed - Polished
20- SAPECADA - Flirting with Freckles ✓
21- PUXA PARA BRANCA - Tending to White ✓
22- BAHIANO - Boy from Bahia ✓
23- CABOCLA - Half Breed → ~~REDBONE~~
~~24- CABO VERDE - Cape Verde~~ Morenão - Big Black Dude
25- COR DE CUIA - Hollow Brown - Gourd-colored
26- COR FIRME - Steady On (sugerimos tirar o Colored, e
deixar apenas a expressão Steady On, que é "Vai Firme") → STEADY
* 27- MESTIÇA - ~~Mestiza~~ - Half Caste   Color
28- PÁLIDA - ~~Pasty~~ ✓ Pale

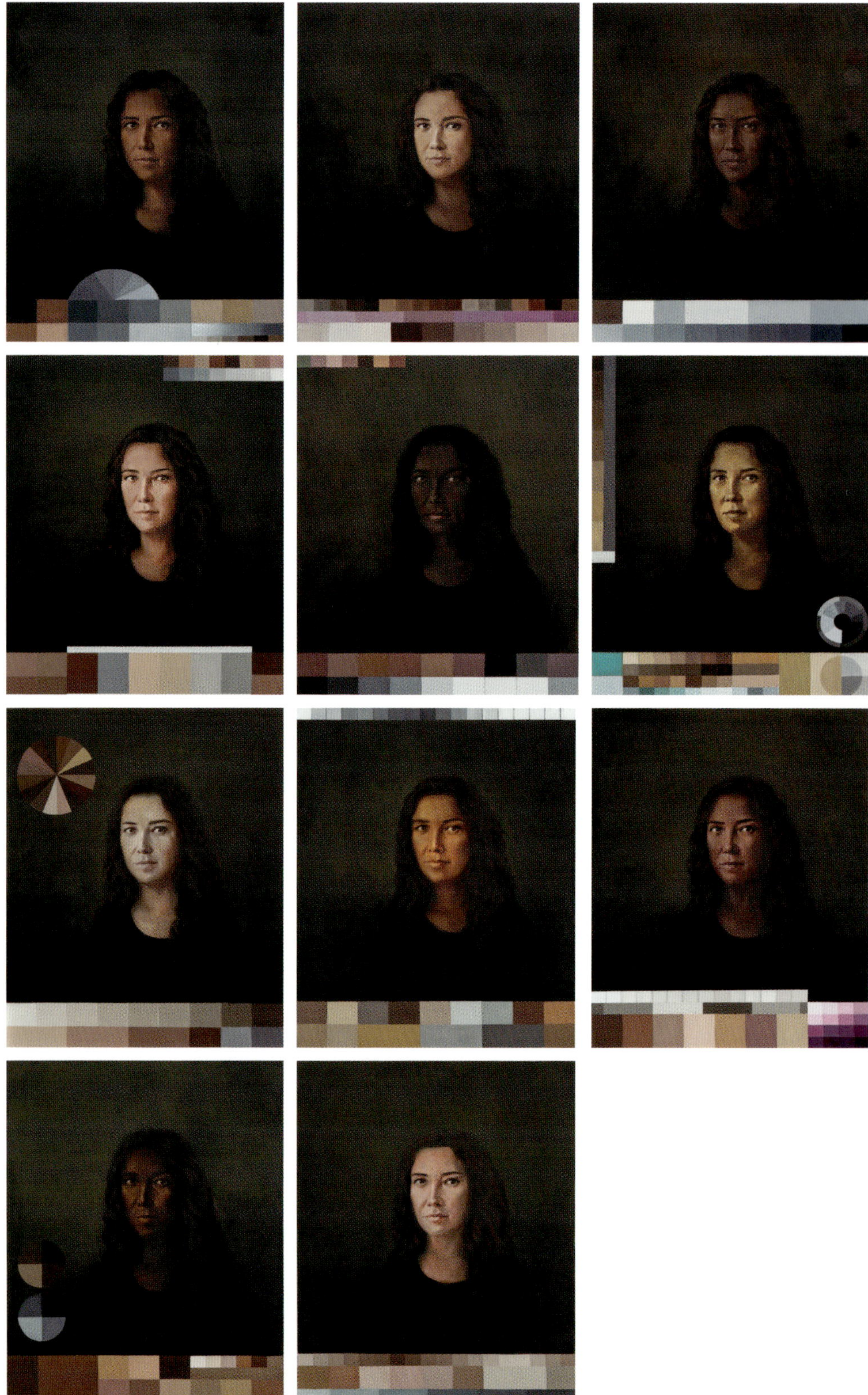

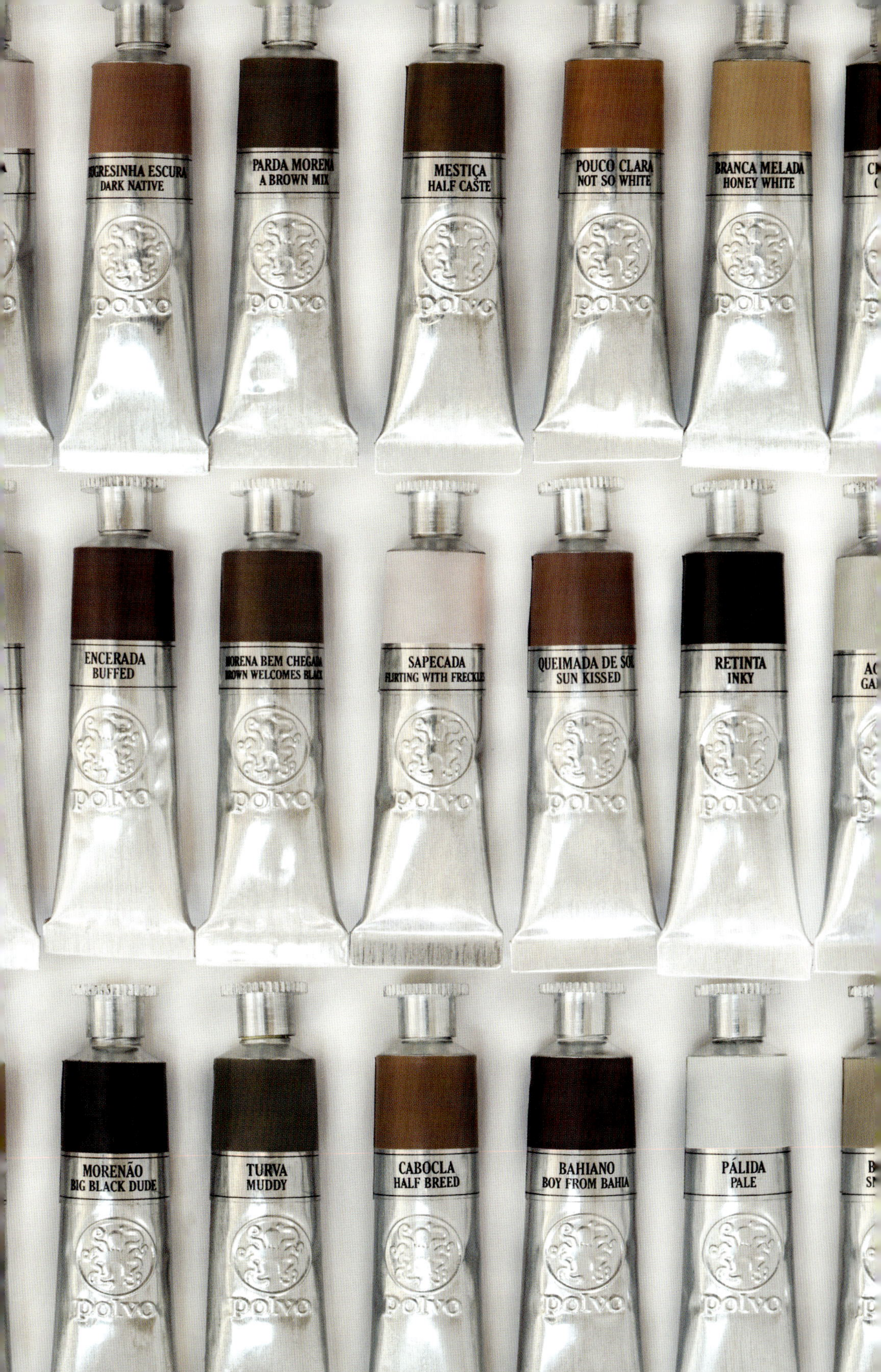
NEGRESINHA ESCURA
DARK NATIVE
PARDA MORENA
A BROWN MIX
MESTIÇA
HALF CAŜTE
POUCO CLARA
NOT SO WHITE
BRANCA MELADA
HONEY WHITE
ENCERADA
BUFFED
MORENA BEM CHEGADA
BROWN WELCOMES BLACK
SAPECADA
FLIRTING WITH FRECKLES
QUEIMADA DE SOL
SUN KISSED
RETINTA
INKY
MORENÃO
BIG BLACK DUDE
TURVA
MUDDY
CABOCLA
HALF BREED
BAHIANO
BOY FROM BAHIA
PÁLIDA
PALE

In paintings, sculpture, photography, and video installations, **ADRIANA VAREJÃO** (b. 1964, Rio de Janeiro, Brazil) presents incisive reflections on the multiplex nature of Brazilian history, memory, and culture. Reflected in her hybridization of mediums in manifold forms— including sculptural paintings and floor-based sculptural works—is the syncretism immanent to Brazil's postcolonial identity. Varejão draws upon aesthetic traditions and a visual legacy resulting from transnational exchange, imperial and otherwise, to create a confluence of forms that she conceives as a metaphor for the modern world.

Tomashi Jackson

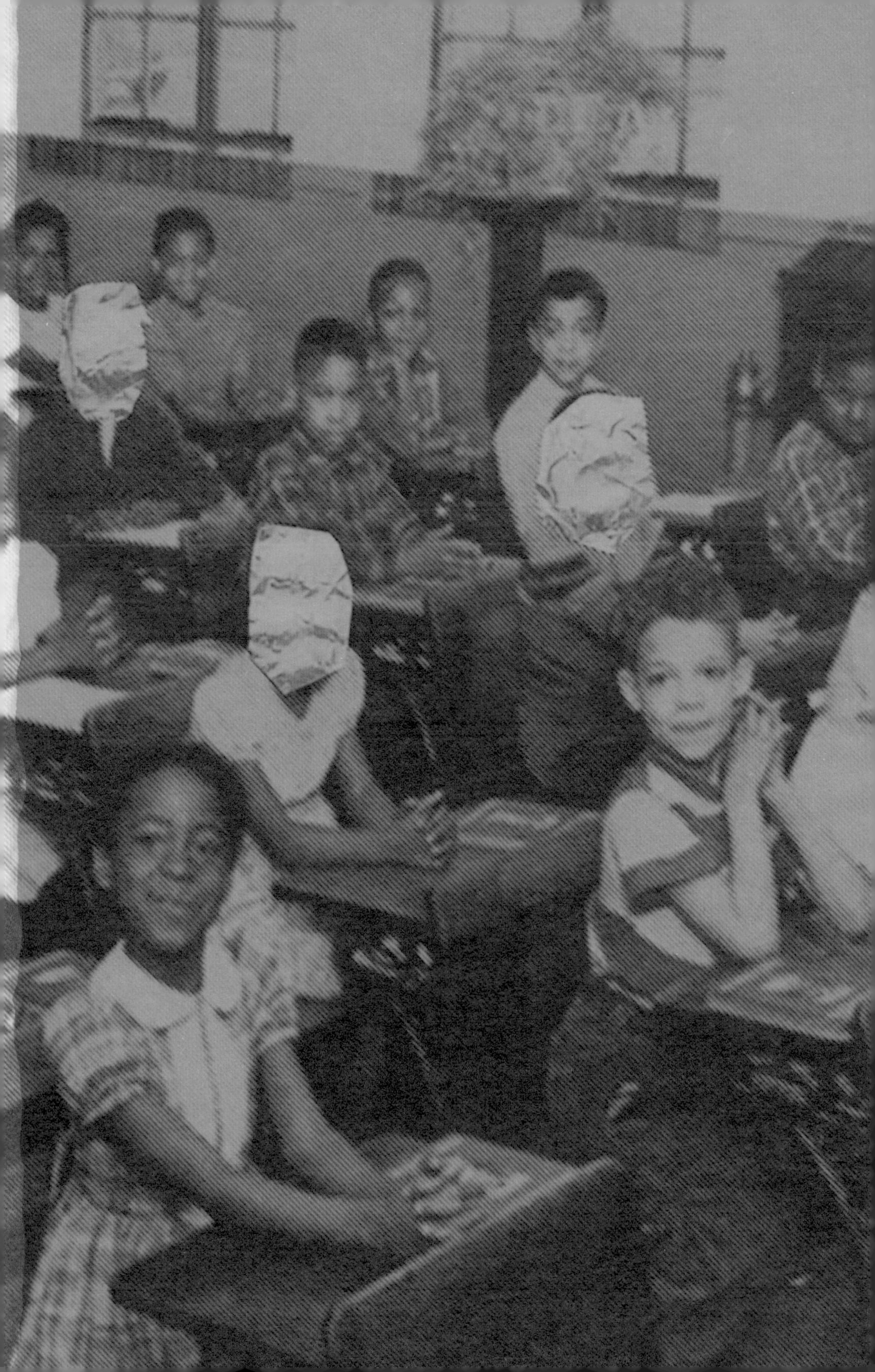

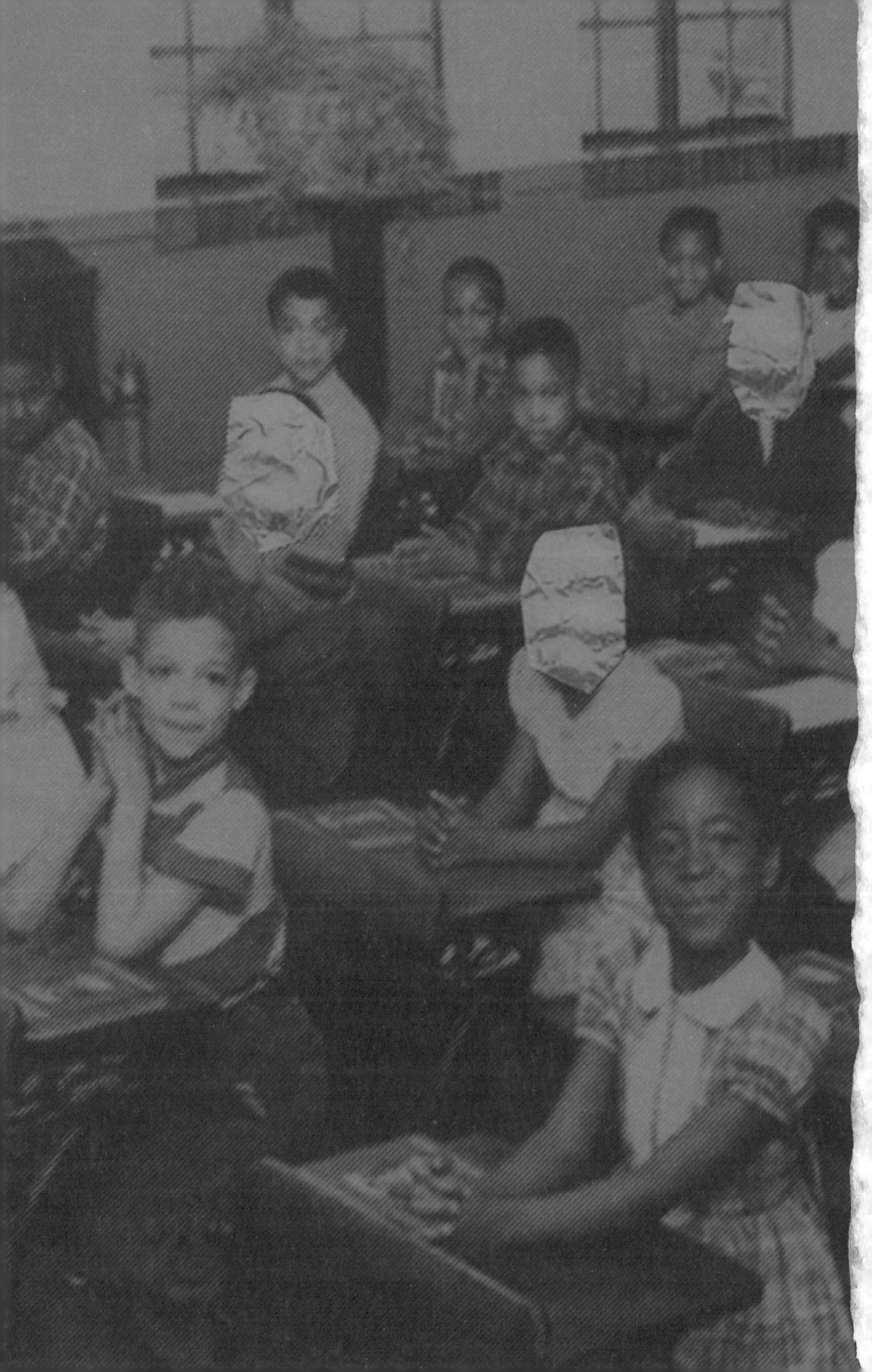

— Regime of gravity —
Ministry of coincidences.
Department (or better):
Regime of Coincidence
Ministry of gravity.
Painting or Sculpture.
Flat container. in glass—[holding]
all sorts of liquids. Colored, pieces
of wood, of iron, chemical reactions.
Shake the container. and look
through it ——

Look for the anti-standard.

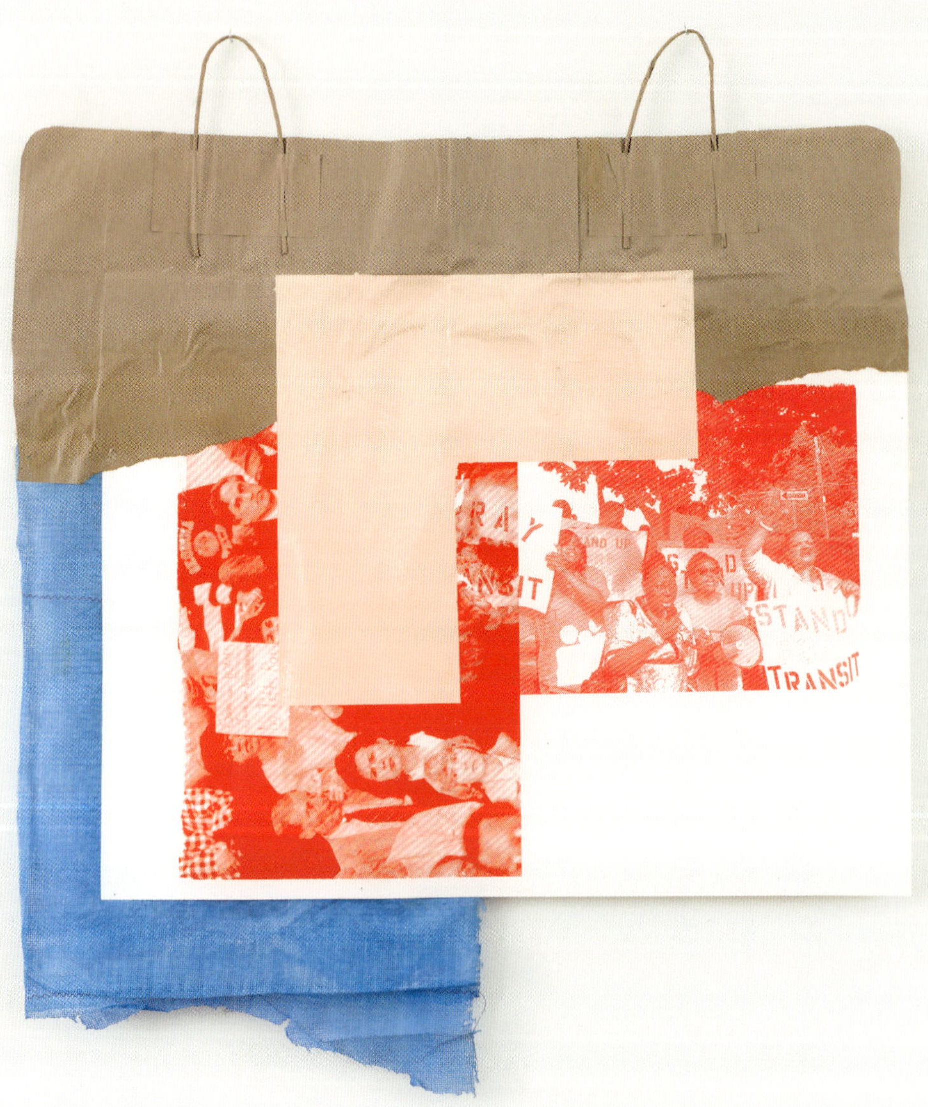

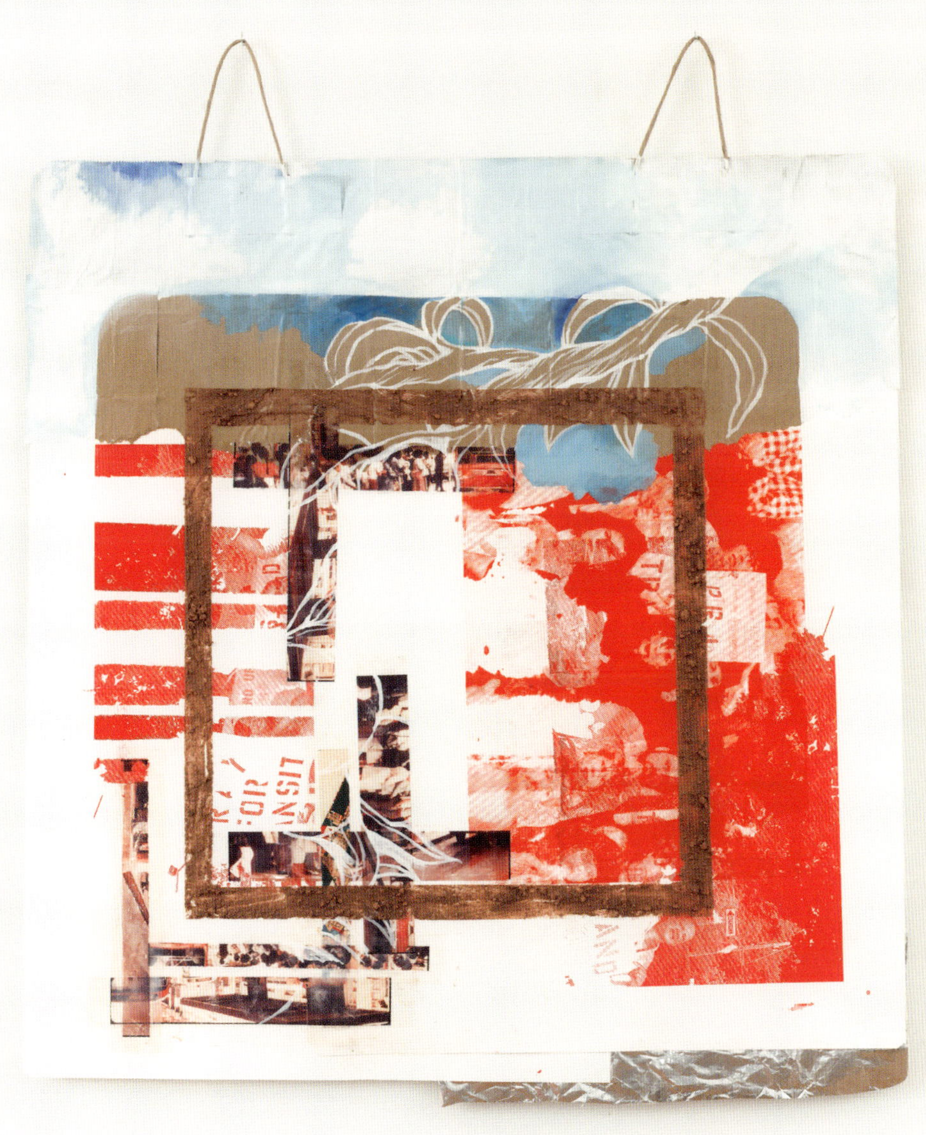

Elements that are not generally recurring.

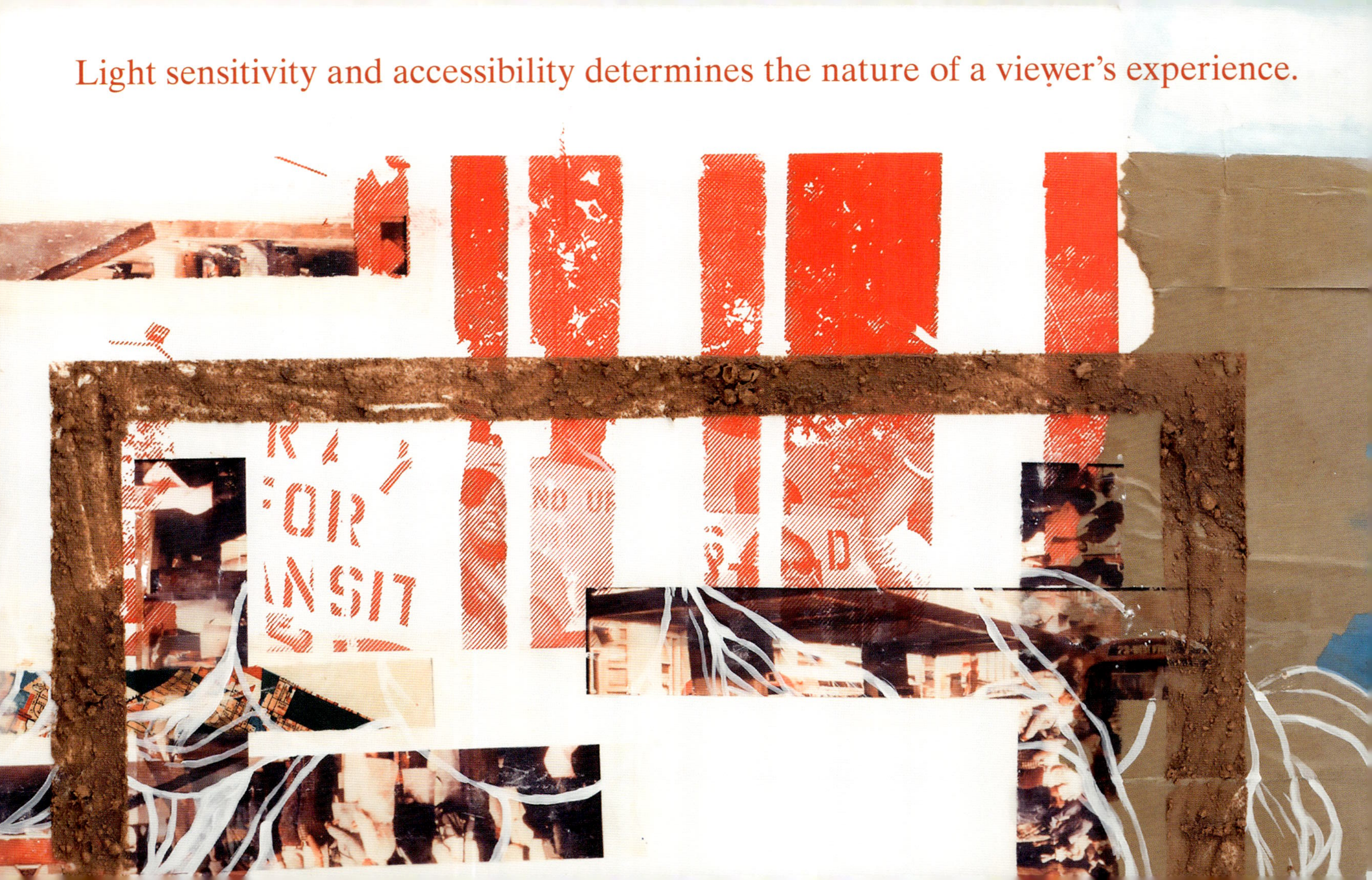
Light sensitivity and accessibility determines the nature of a viewer's experience.

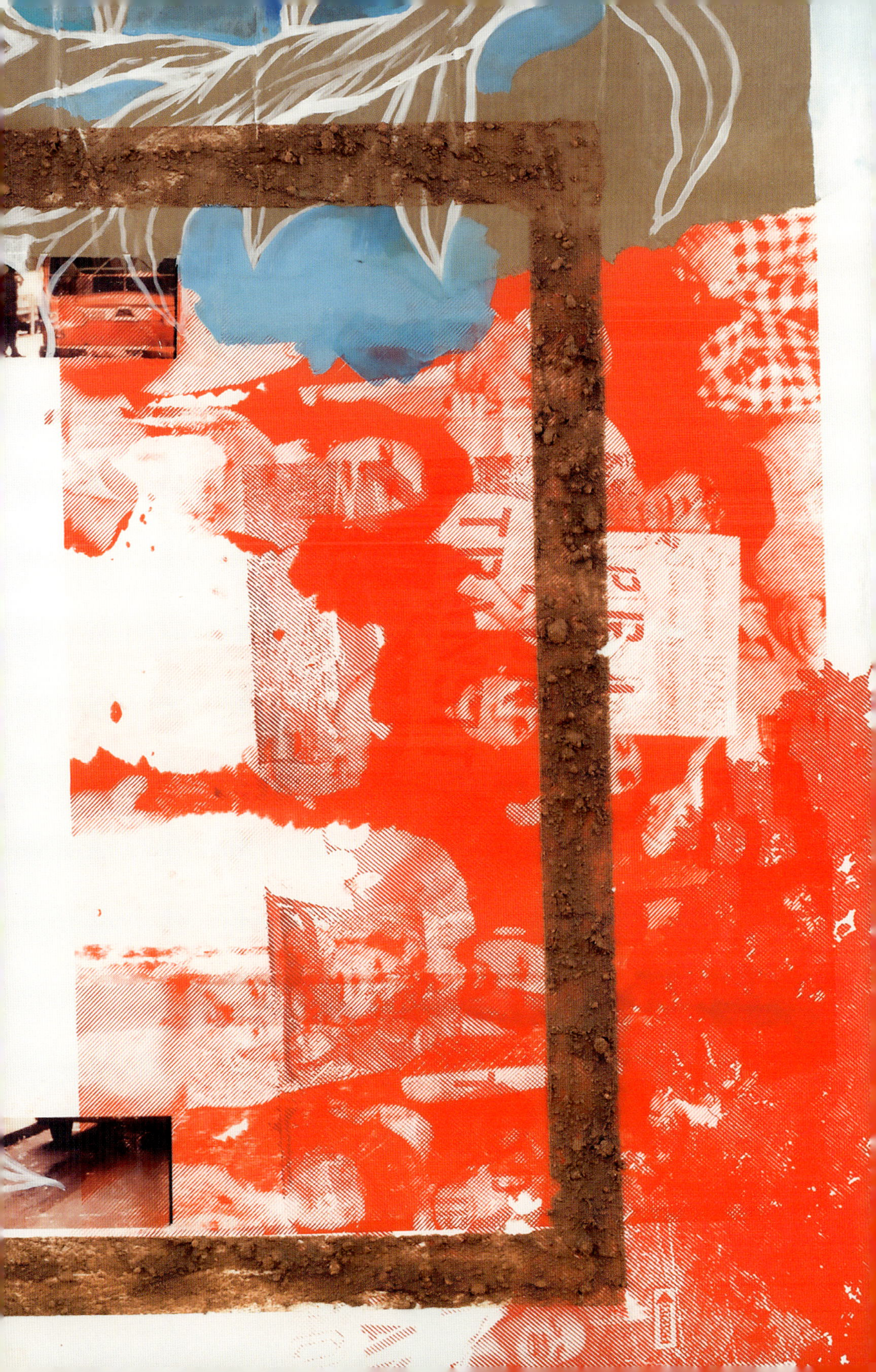

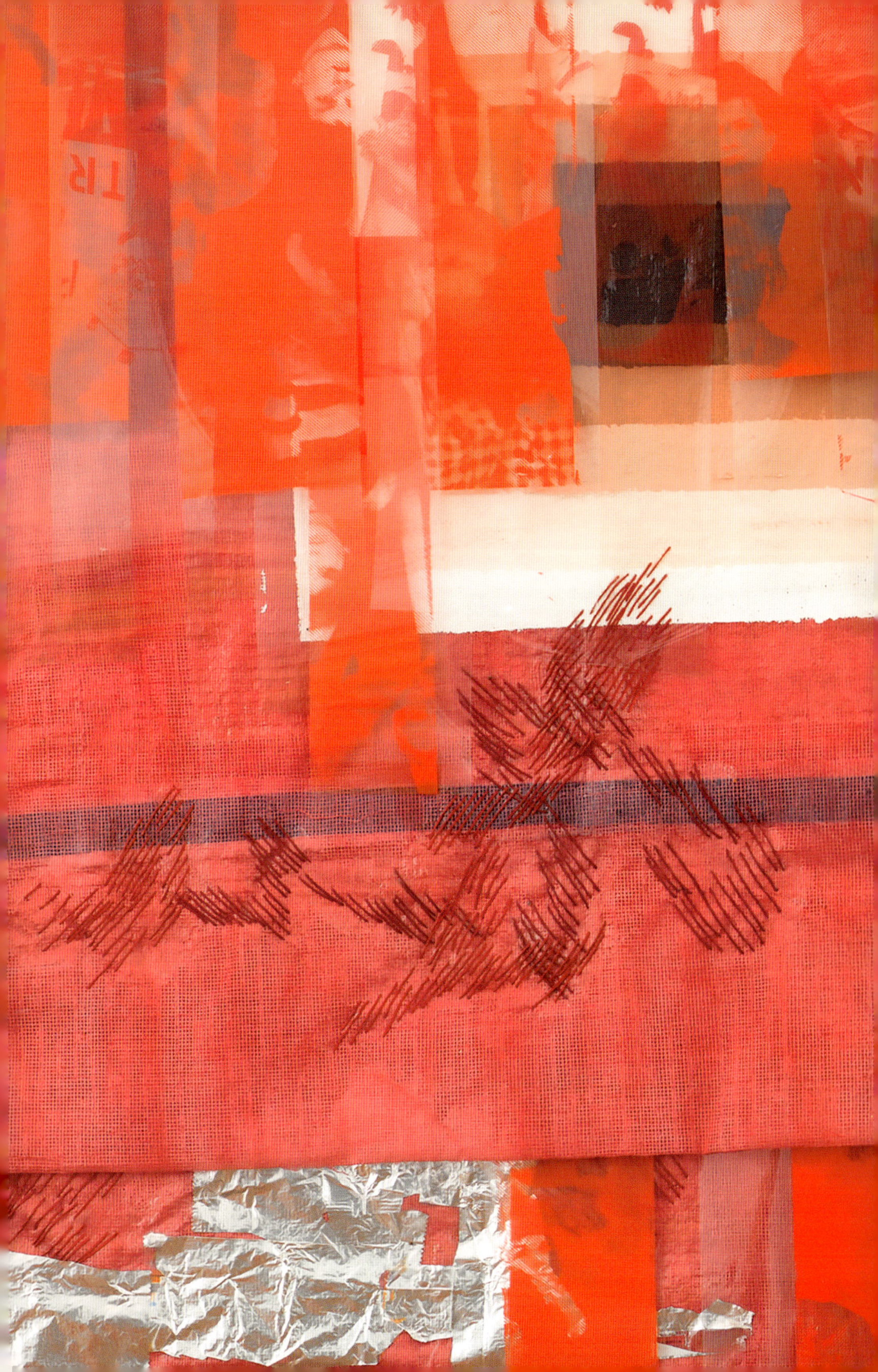

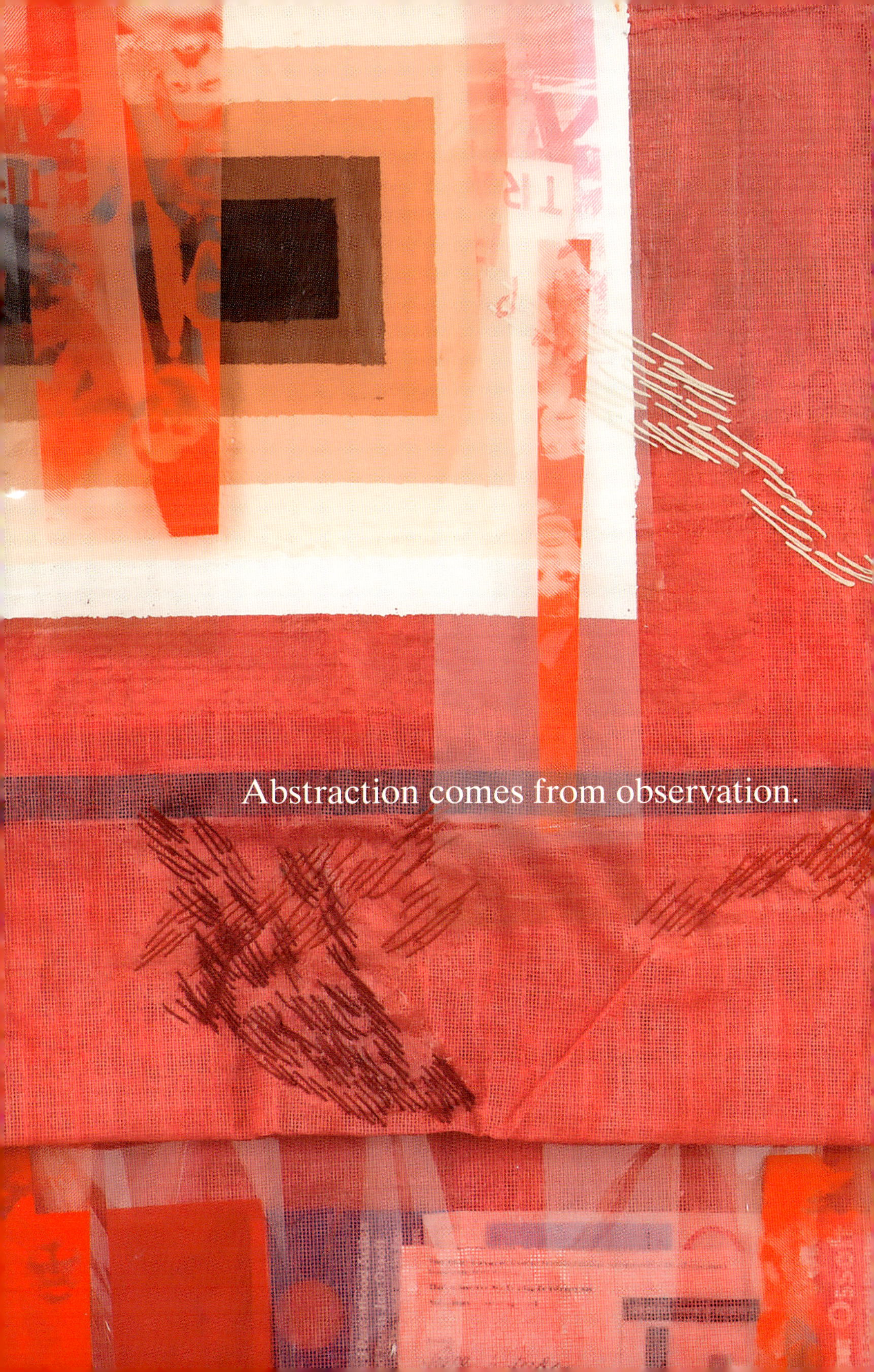
Abstraction comes from observation.

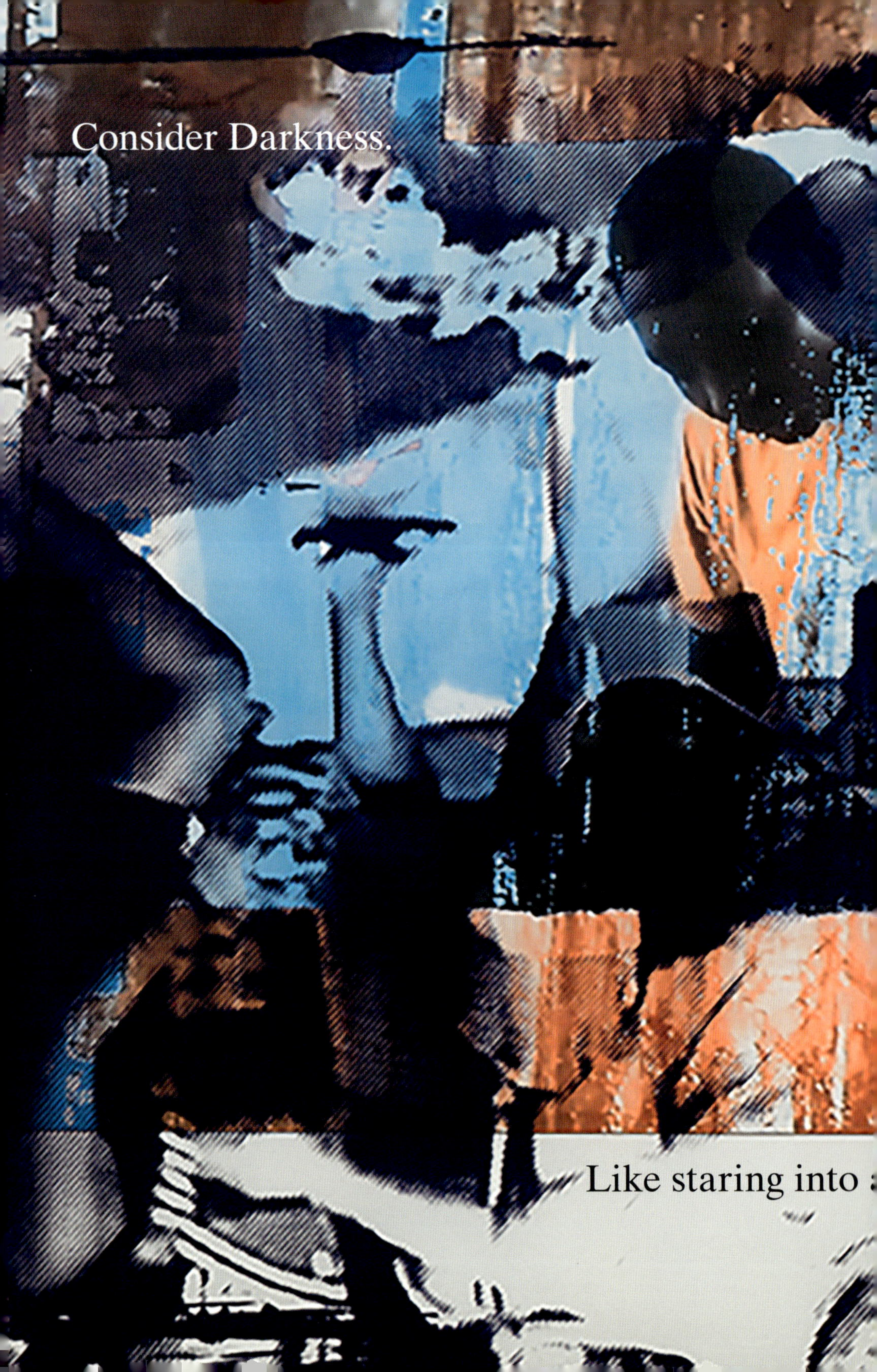
Consider Darkness.
Like staring into

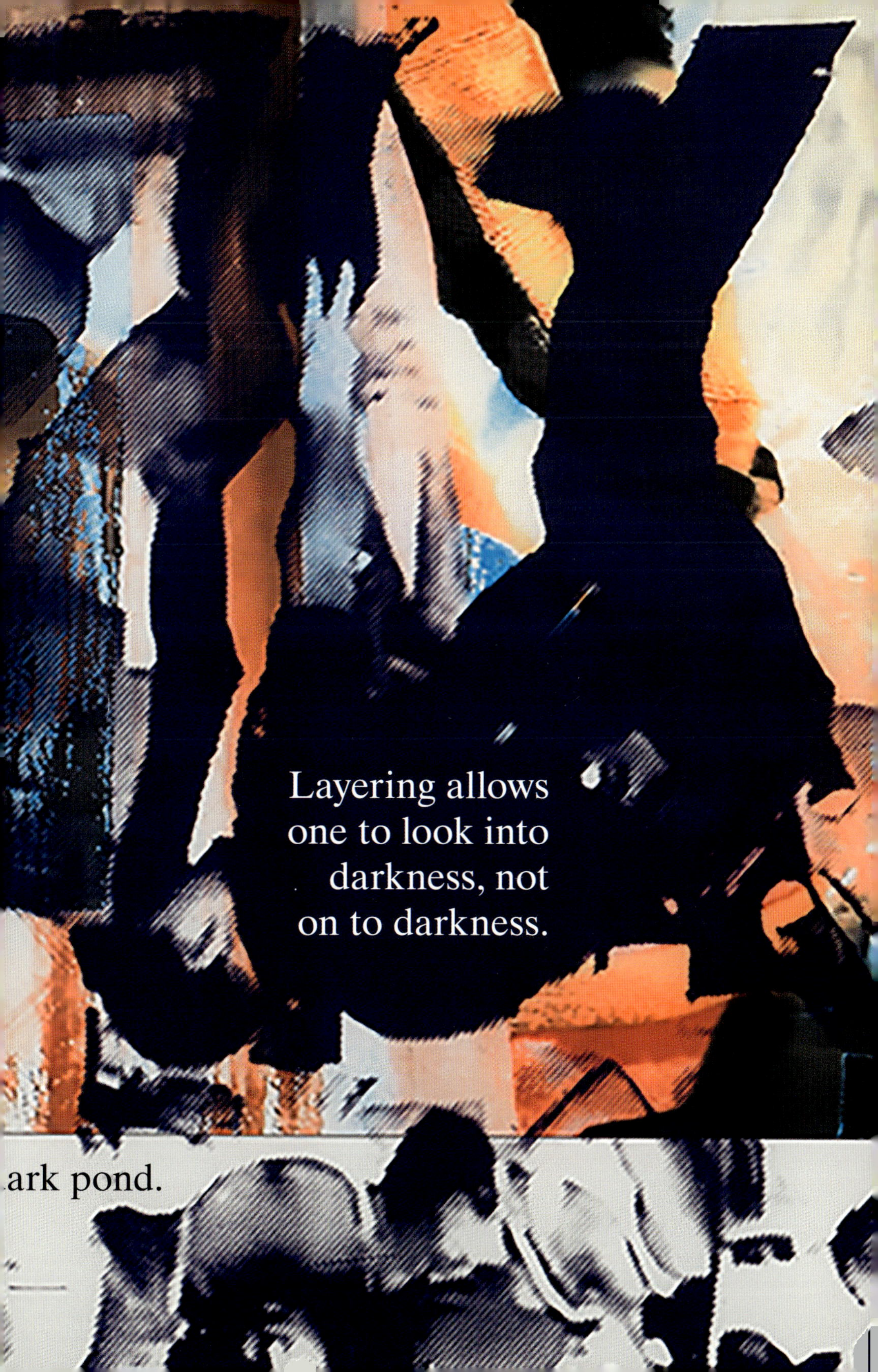
Layering allows
one to look into
darkness, not
on to darkness.
ark pond.

TOMASHI JACKSON (b. 1980, Houston, United States) is a multi-disciplinary artist who uses the formal properties of color perception as an aesthetic strategy to investigate the value of human life in public space. As a painter studying color theory, Jackson observed that the language used to describe the formal interaction of colors echoed the language found in United States public policy documents and court proceedings regarding issues of public concern—including education, transportation, and housing. Jackson's interrogation of shared languages of color, in reference to chromatic or social phenomena, creates a narrative framework from which she constructs her own language of abstraction for her videos, paintings, collages, and photographs.

Sarah Crowner

Specifications for "Readymades".

  by planning for a moment

to come (on such a day, such

a date such a minute), "to inscribe

a readymade".— The readymade

can later

be looked for. (with all kinds of delays)
             then
  The important thing is just

this matter of timing, this snapshot effect, like

a speech delivered on no matter
         but
what occasion at such and such an hour.

It is a kind of rendezvous.

— Naturally inscribe that date,
        on the readymade
hour, minute, as information.

---

  also the serial characteristic

of the readymade.

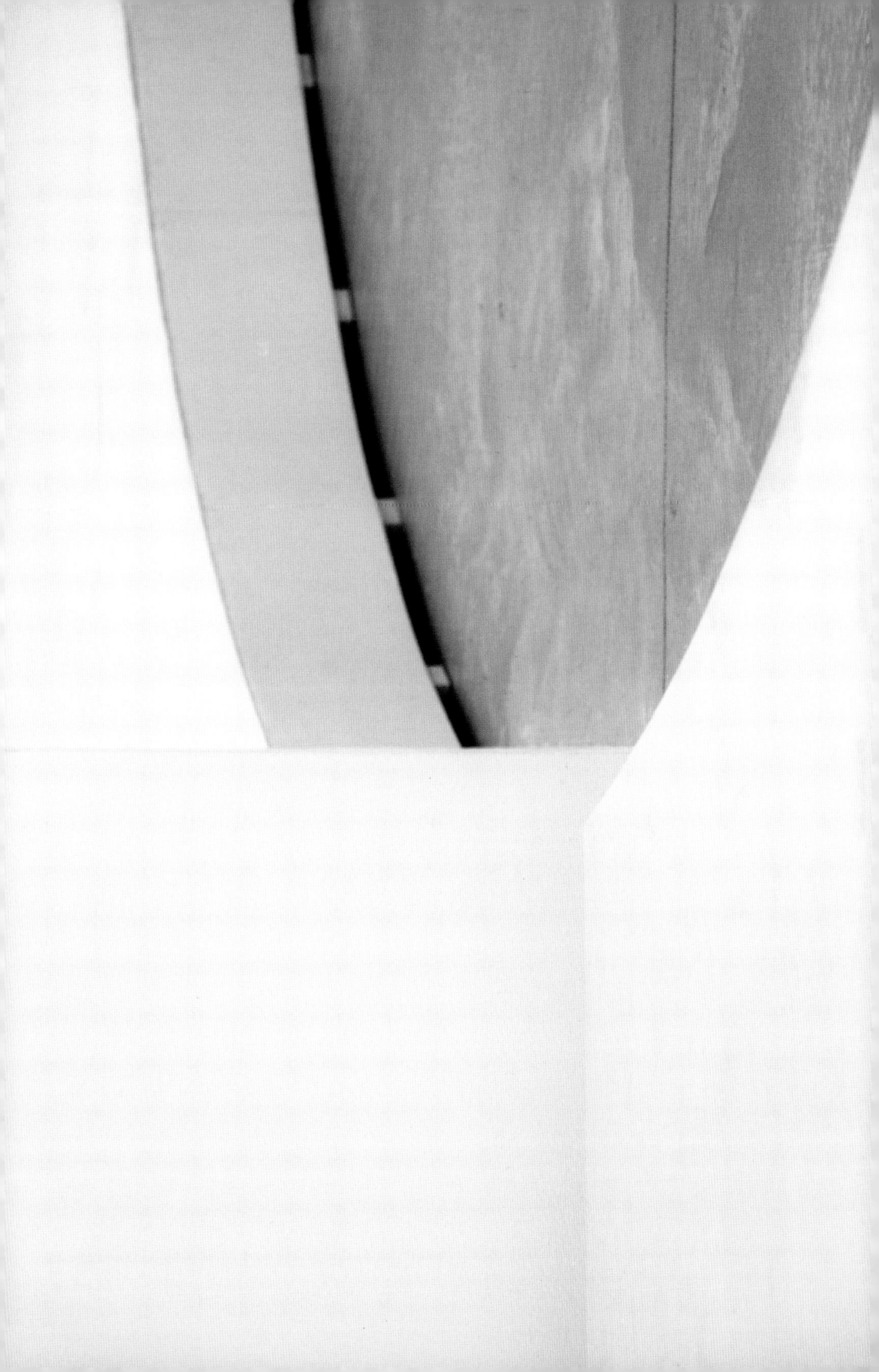

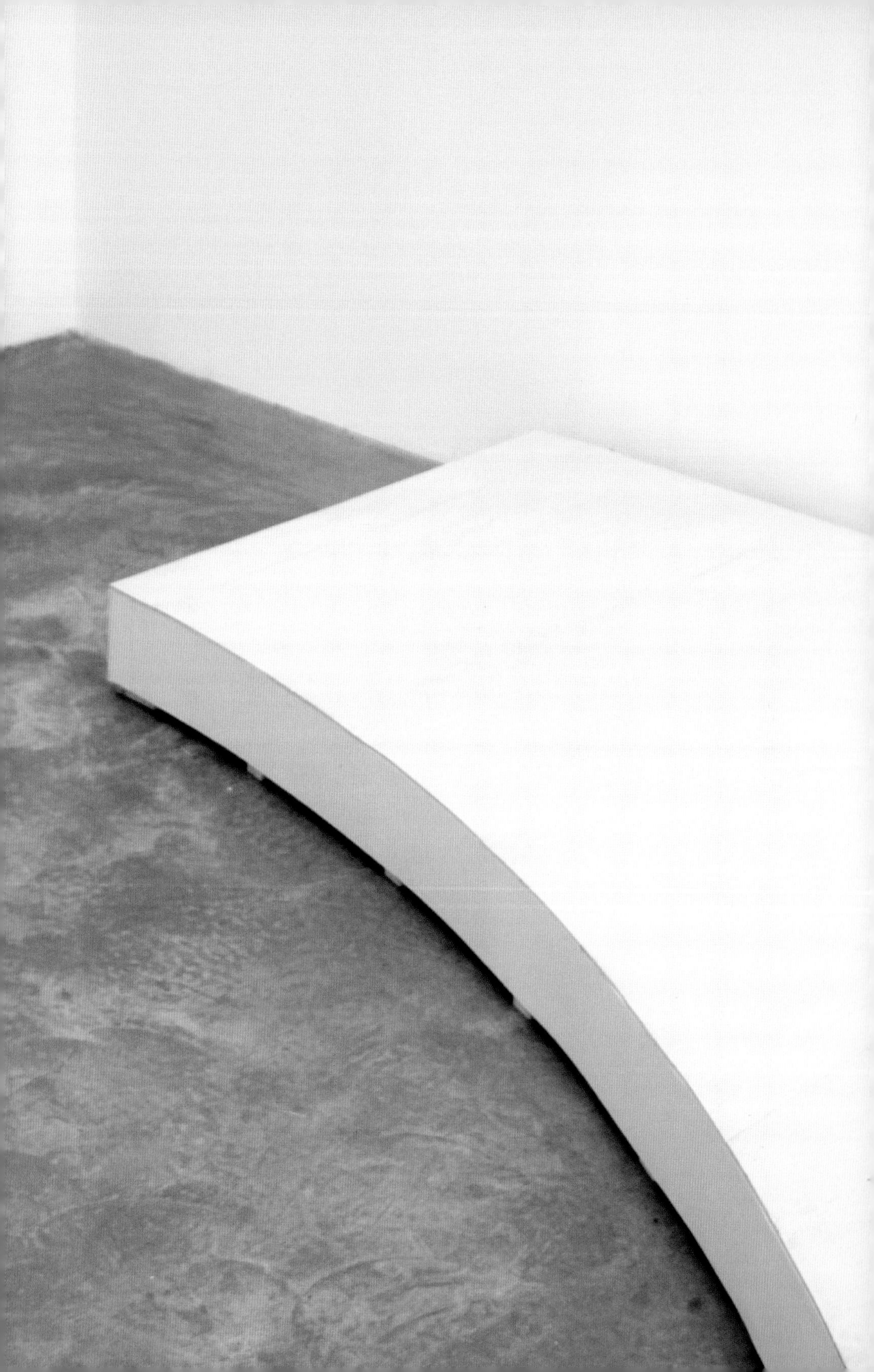

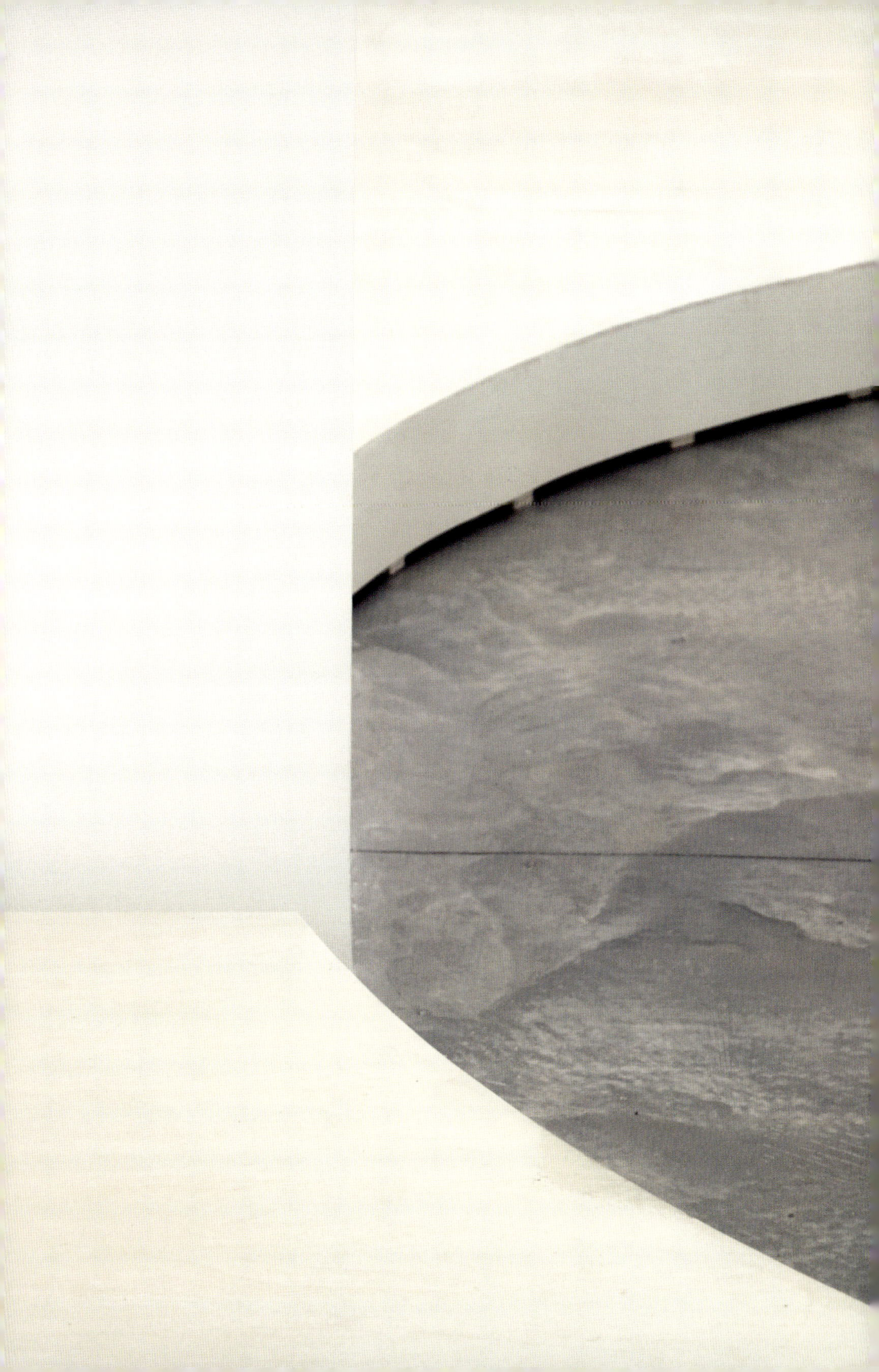

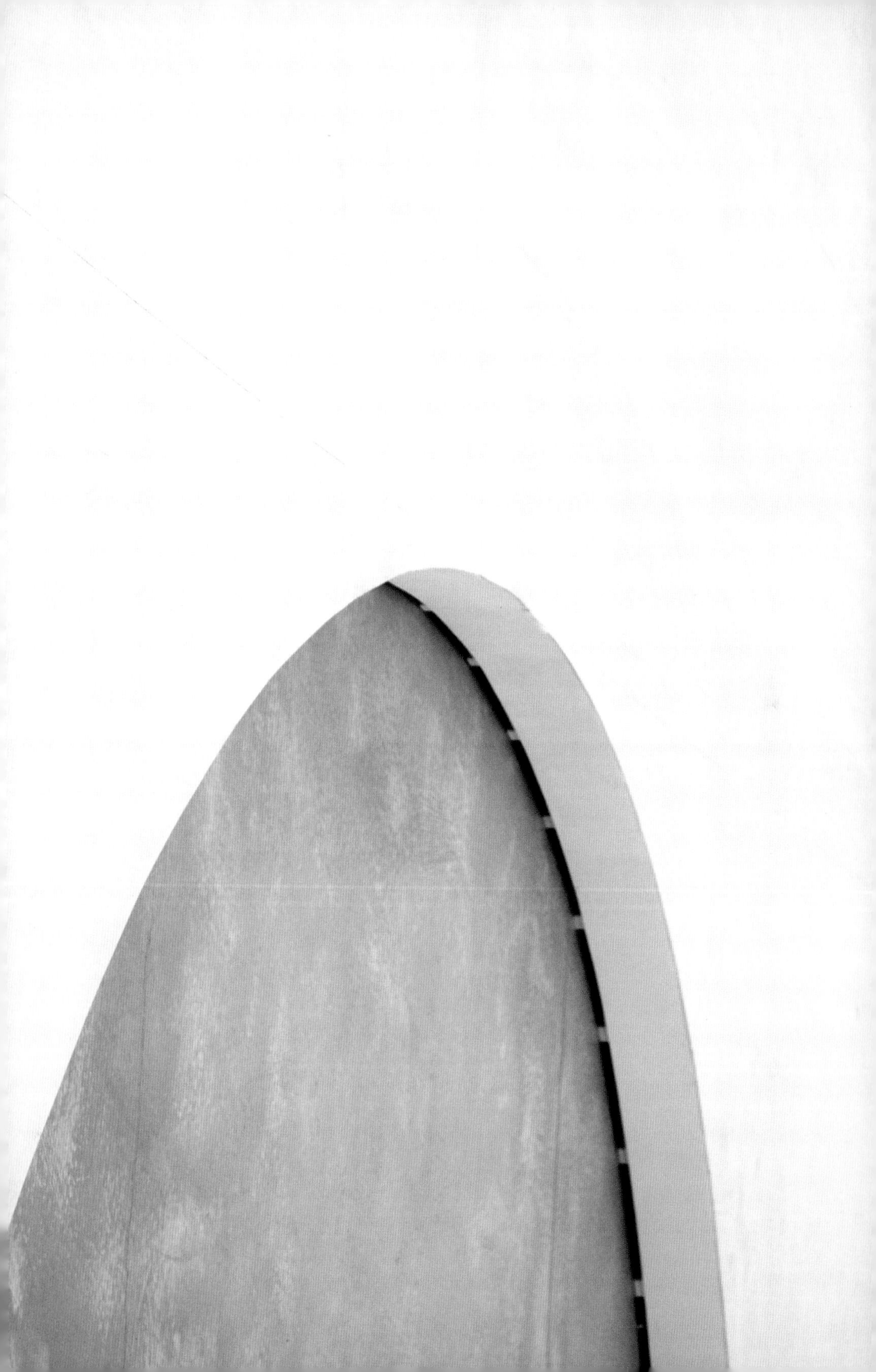

SARAH CROWNER's (b. 1974, Philadelphia, United States) diverse practice ranges from paintings and ceramics to sculpture and theater curtains. Her bold and colorful paintings and tile works incorporate forms found in architecture, nature, and in the history of twentieth-century art and design. Her stitched paintings are created by using an industrial sewing machine to sew painted and raw irregular panels of canvas together, simultaneously revealing the painting's composition and construction. Sections are painted in saturated primary colors to imply a form, a presence, a possibility. The stitched seams remain visible, like plant veins or arteries, reflecting her interest in systems and patterns, production and reproduction, in culture and nature. In recent years Crowner has exhibited her paintings in conjunction with ceramic tile murals and floor installations on elevated platforms, creating a bespoke, intimate environment and stage. Crowner embraces the idea of paintings as object and her works embody the experience of architecture and space both within themselves and their display. Her work draws attention to the surrounding context, from the painted walls, brick patterns, concrete floors, or plate glass windows. These dynamic three-dimensional abstractions seductively speak to connection, opposition, separation, hierarchy, transition, and assimilation.

Claudia Wieser

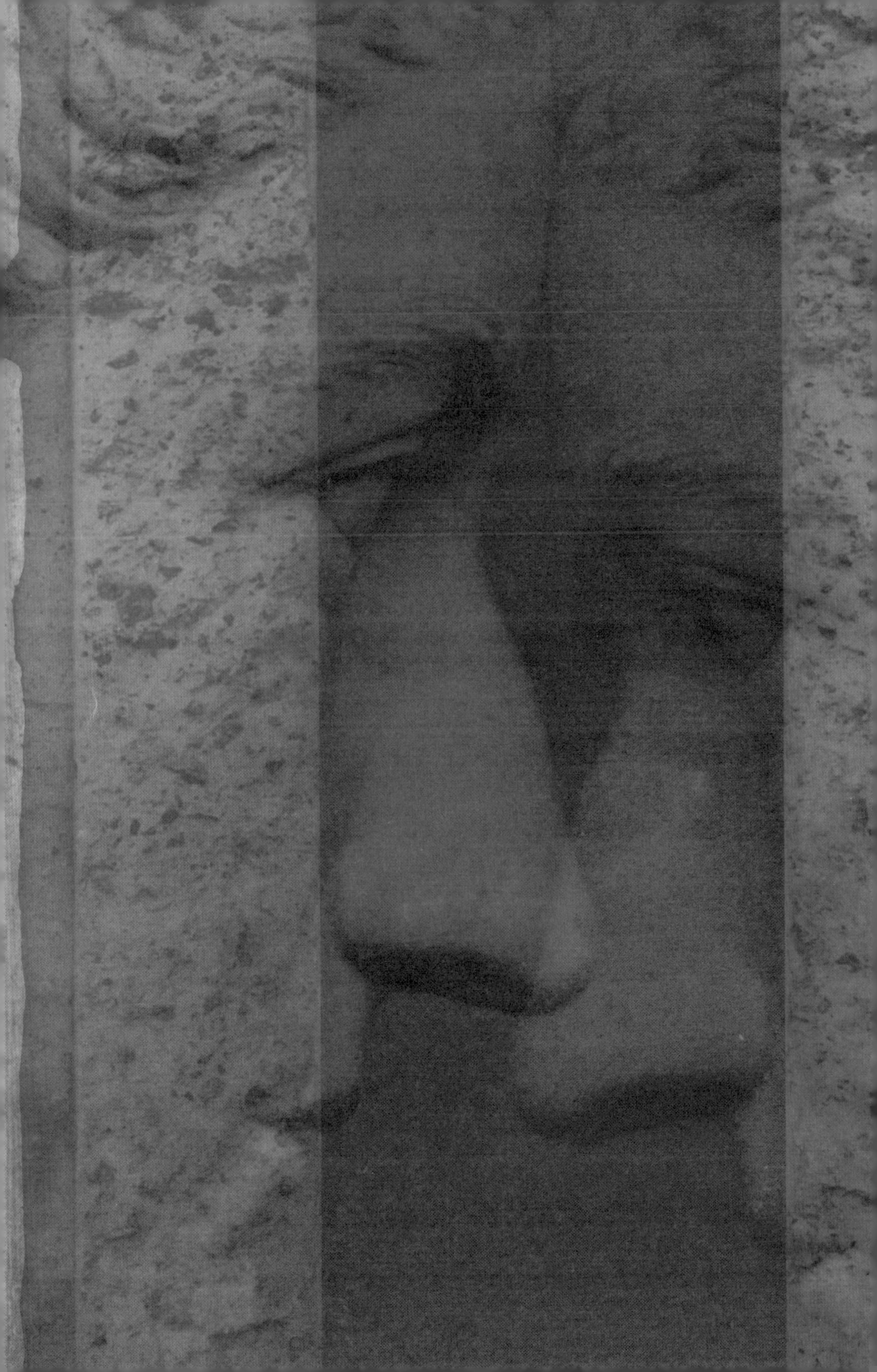

                                   identifying
To lose the possibility of <u>recognizing</u>

<u>2 similar objects</u> —

                2 colors, 2 laces

2 hats, 2 forms whatsoever

to reach the Impossibility of
                        <u>visual</u>
                sufficient memory,

to transfer

from one

                like object to another

the <u>memory</u> imprint

———— Same possibility

with sounds; with brain facts

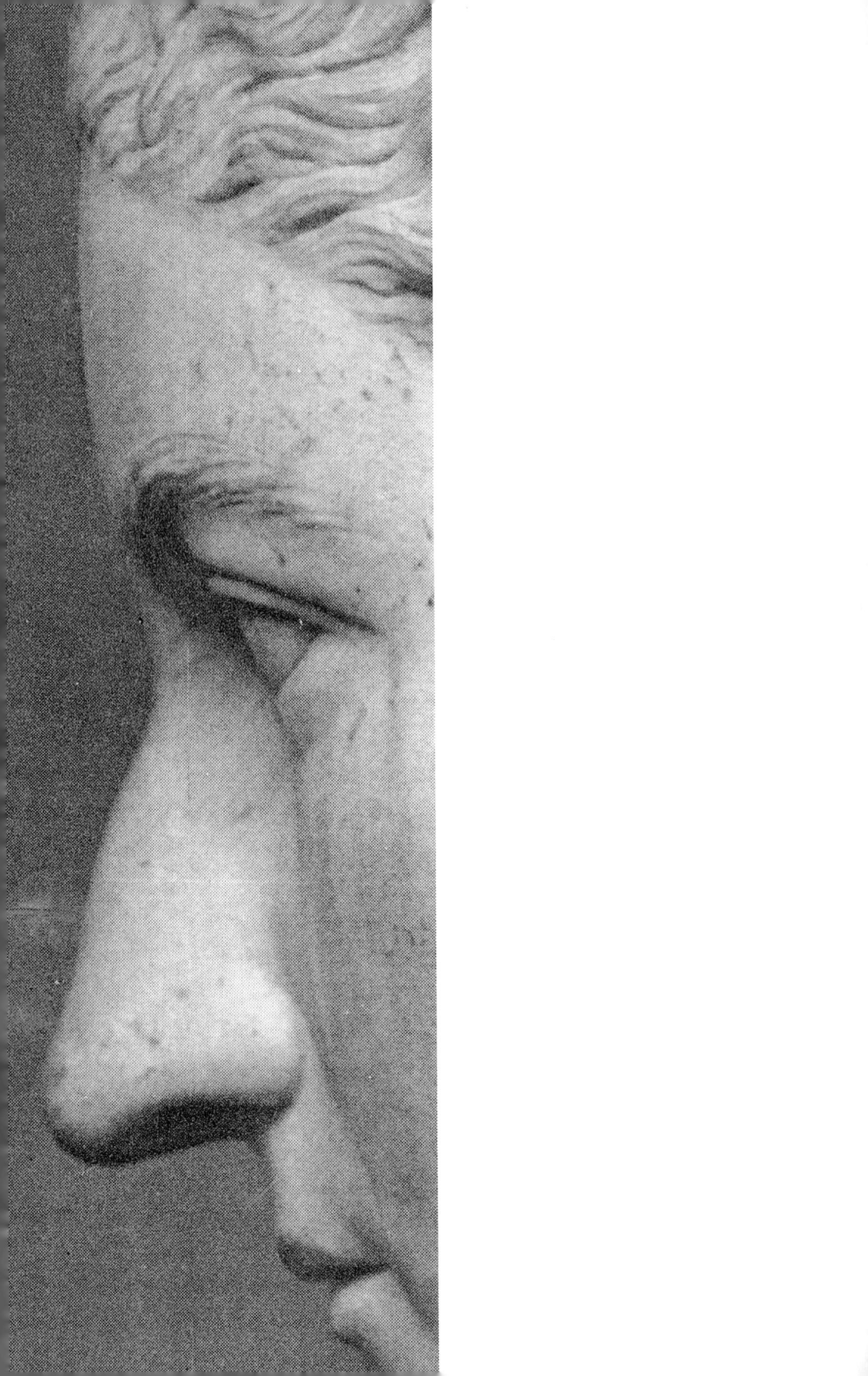

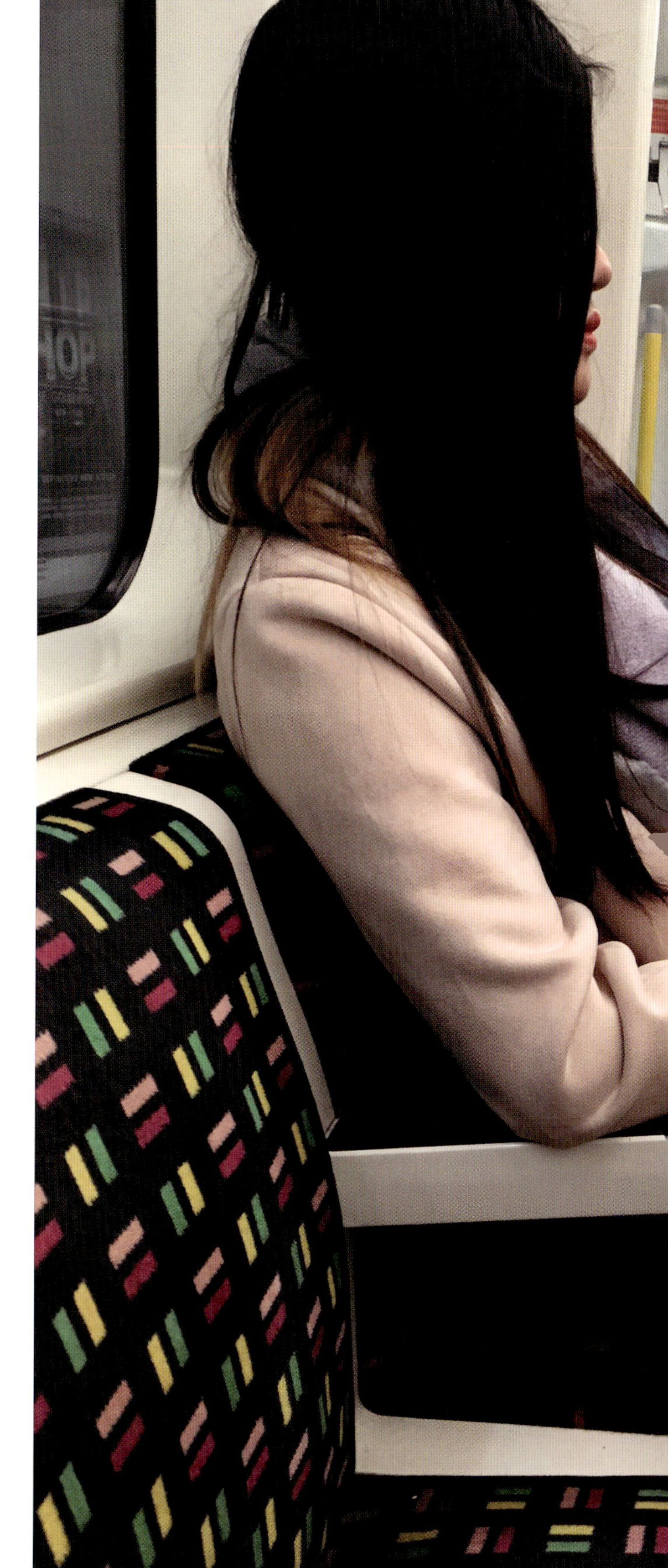

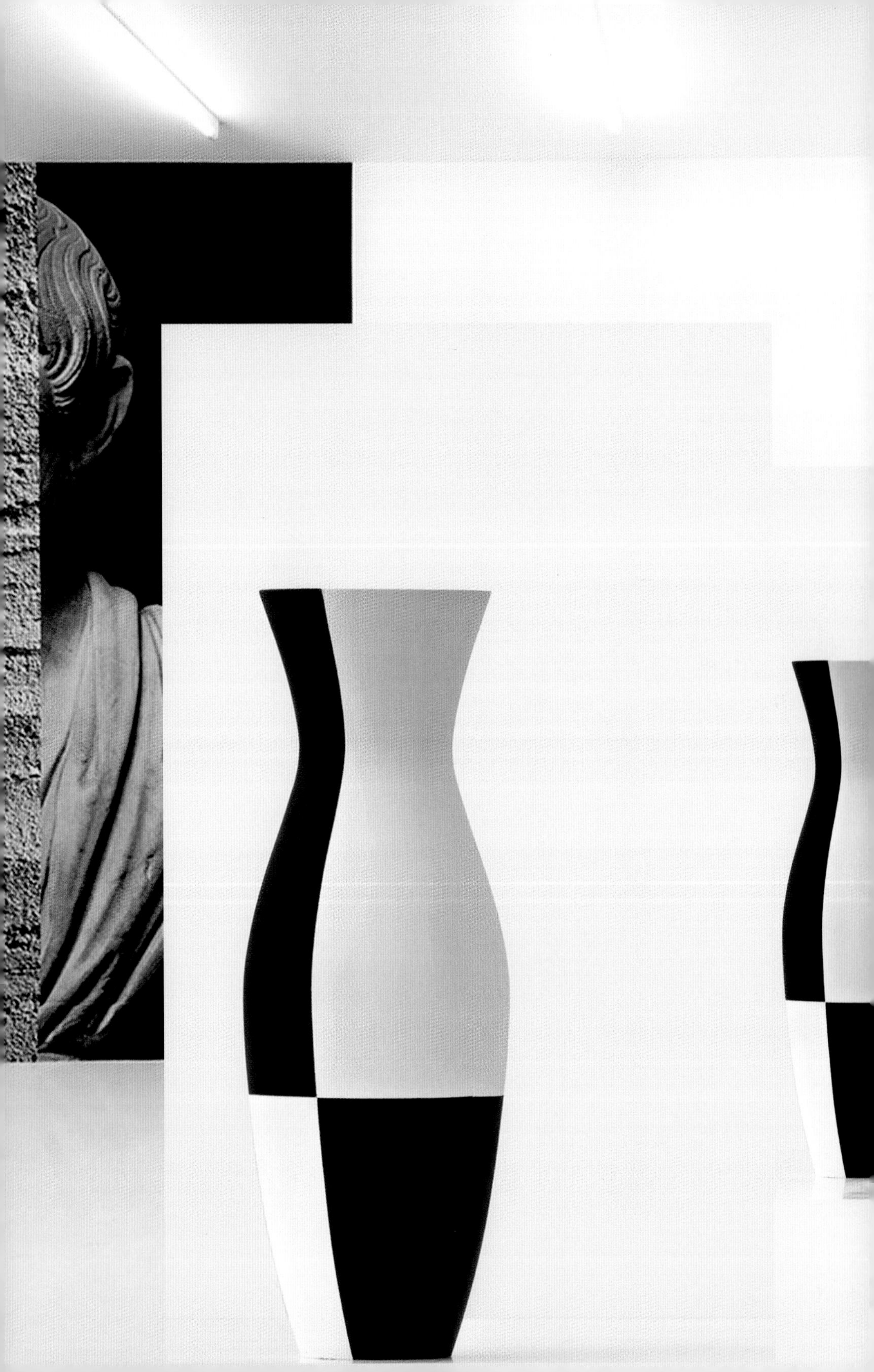

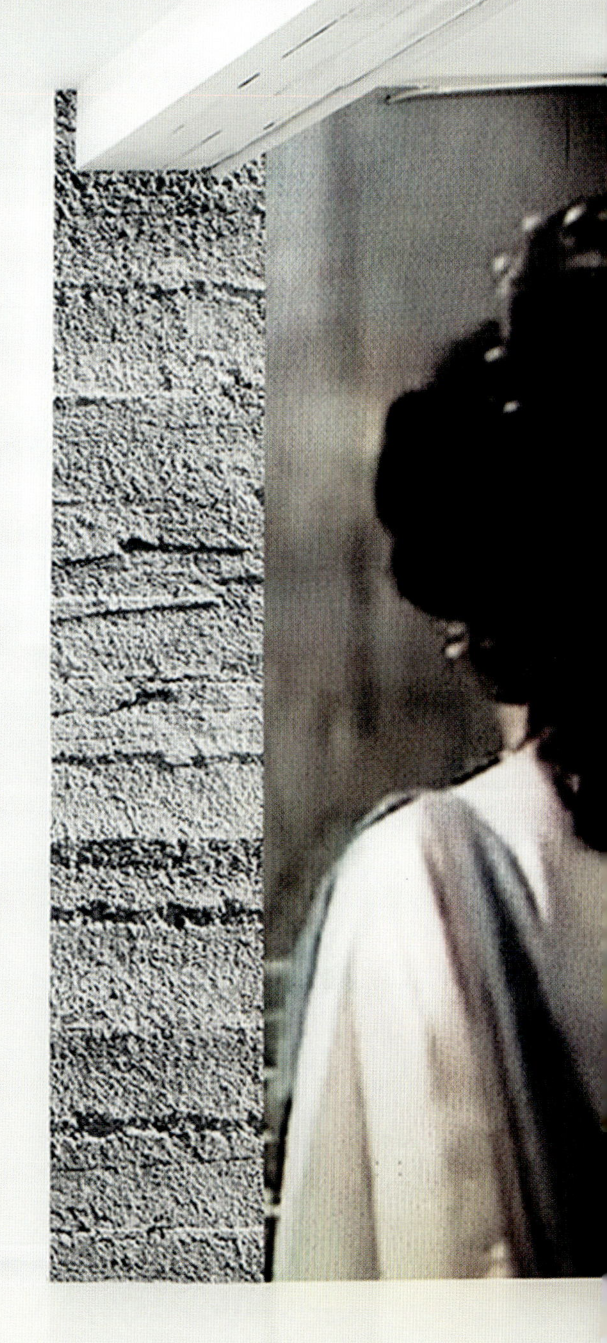

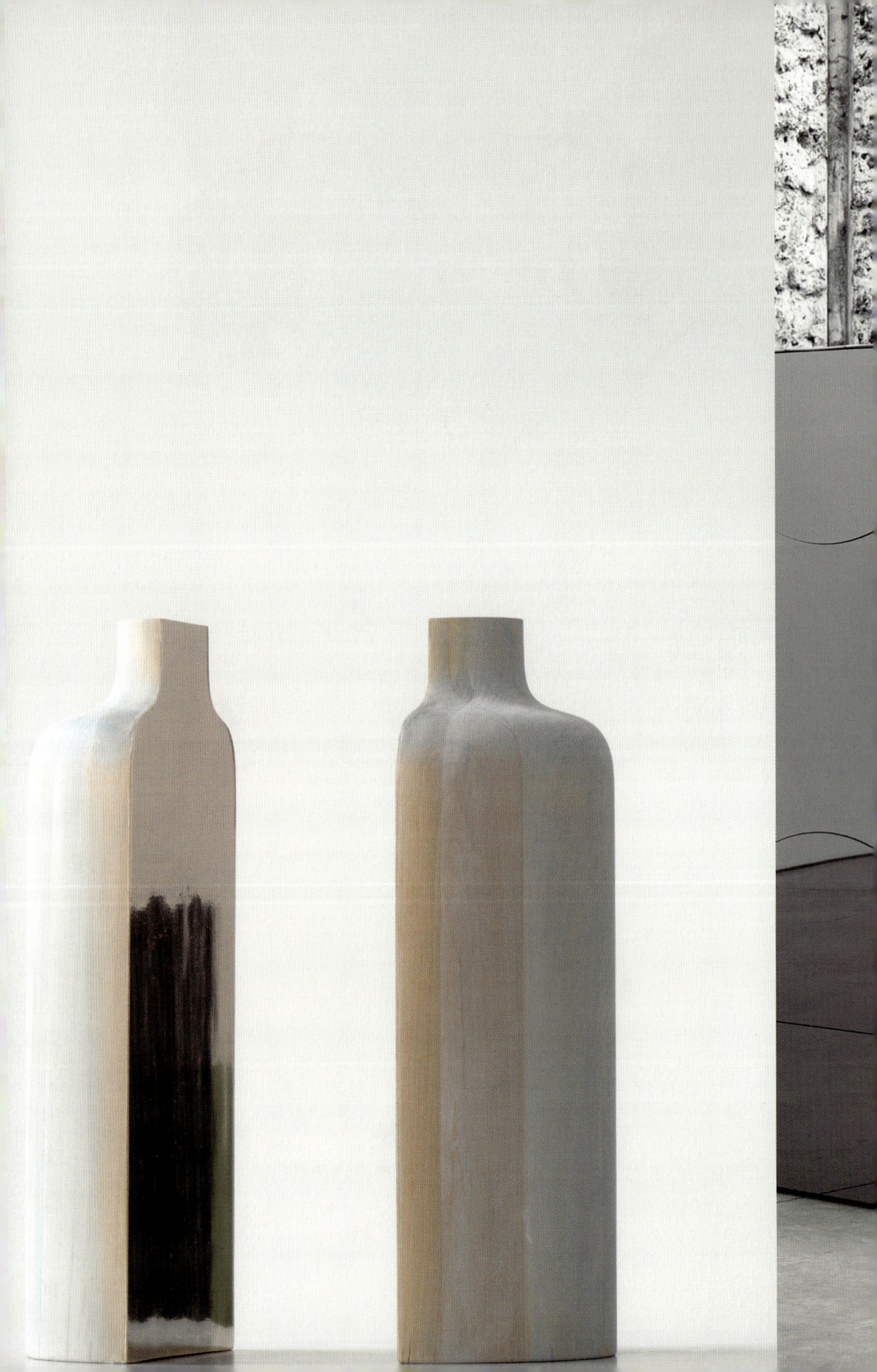

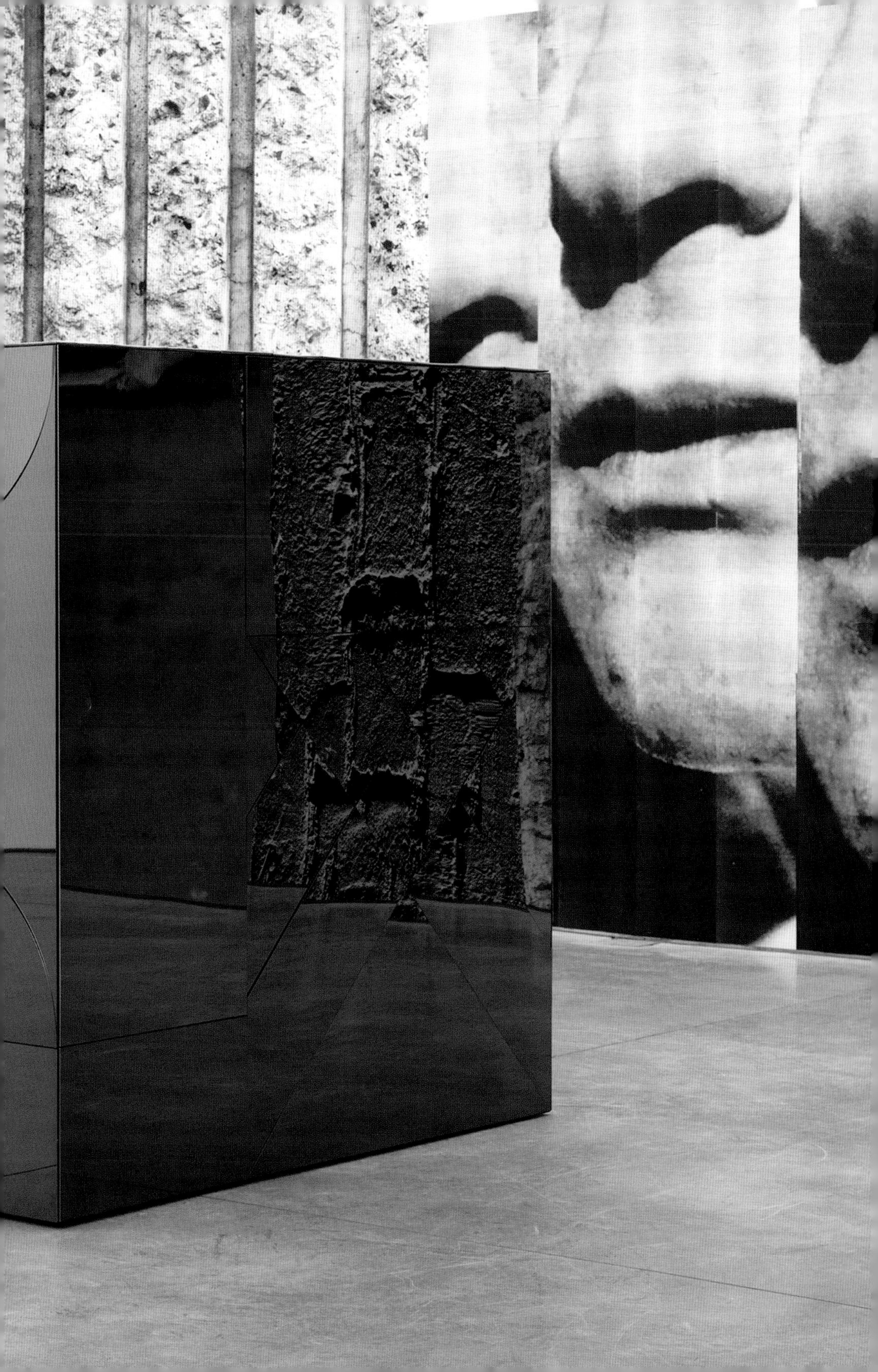

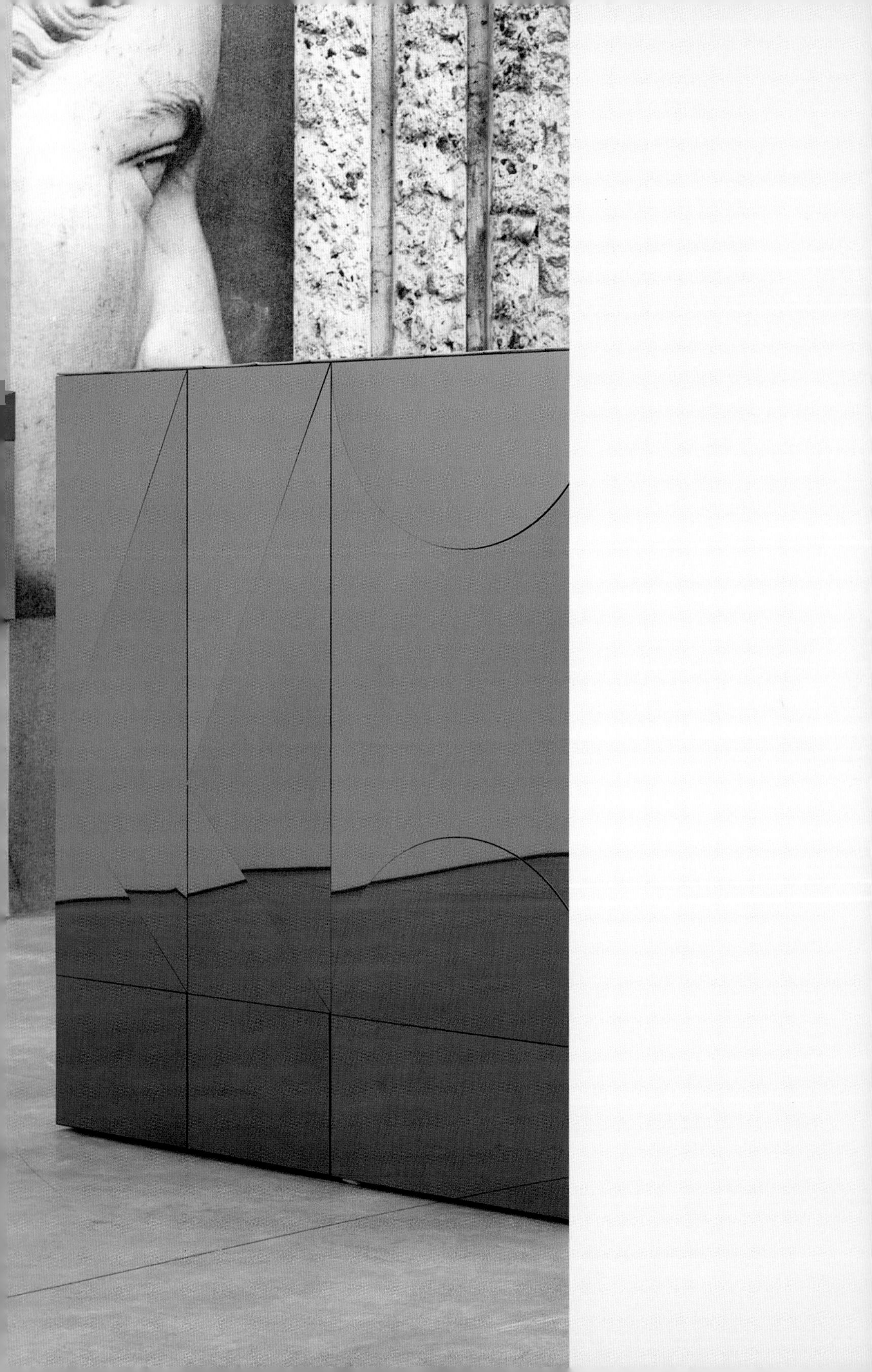

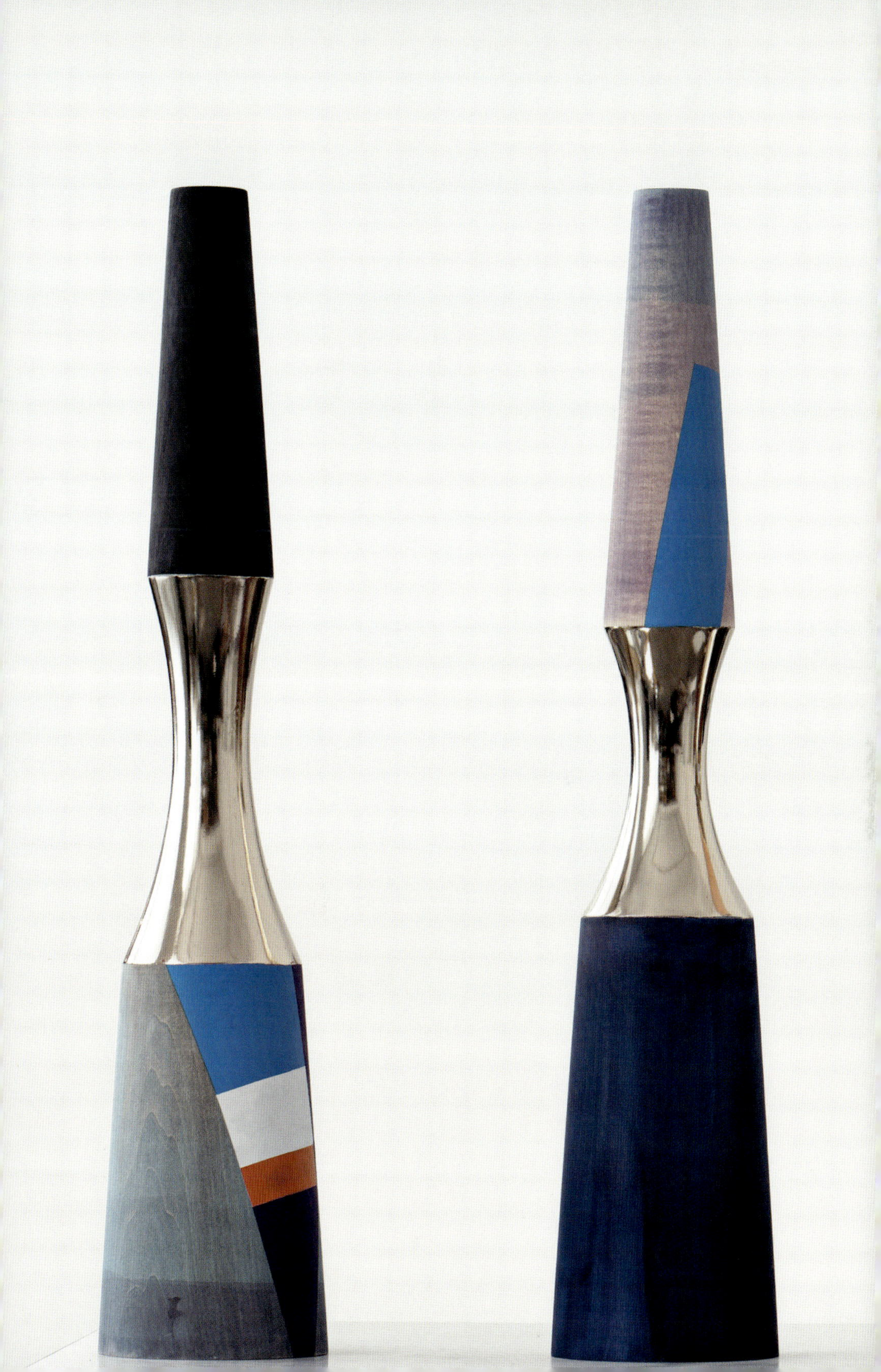

CLAUDIA WIESER (b. 1973, Freilassing, Germany) is known for her modernist-inspired geometric constructions. Influenced by the work of Wassily Kandinsky and Paul Klee, artists who embraced spirituality in their aesthetic process, Wieser broadens their ideals to consider abstractions's coexistence with physiological experience. Her hand is readily evident in a multimedia process that is both meticulous and delicate. Through an early apprenticeship as a blacksmith at Bergmeister Kunstschmiede, Wieser honed her understanding of art and the object, the aesthetic and the functional. This studied craft informs her approach to the technical drafting of her multi-faceted mirrors, hand-painted and patterned ceramics, and carved wooden sculpture.

Julia Dault

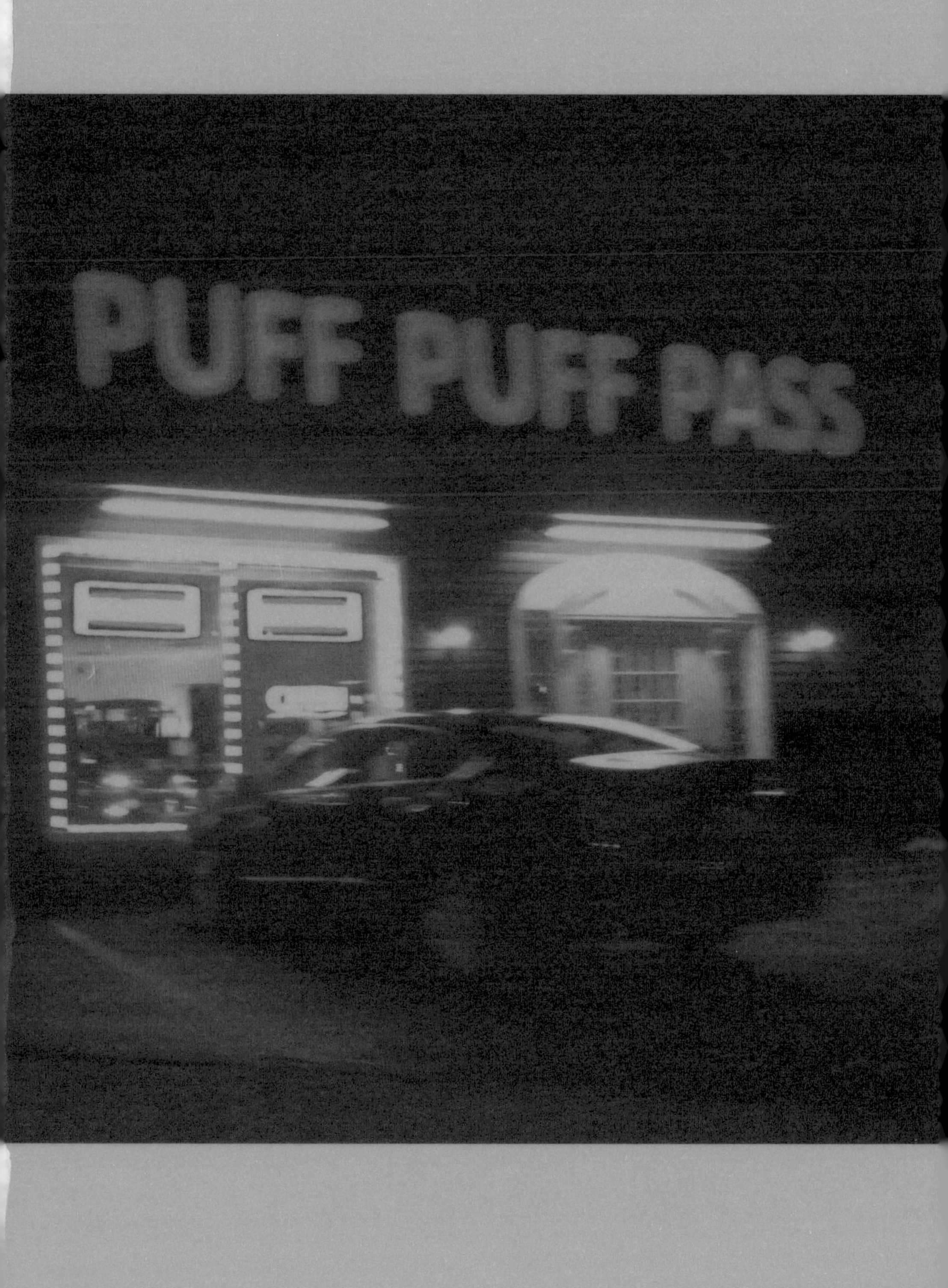
PUFF PUFF PASS

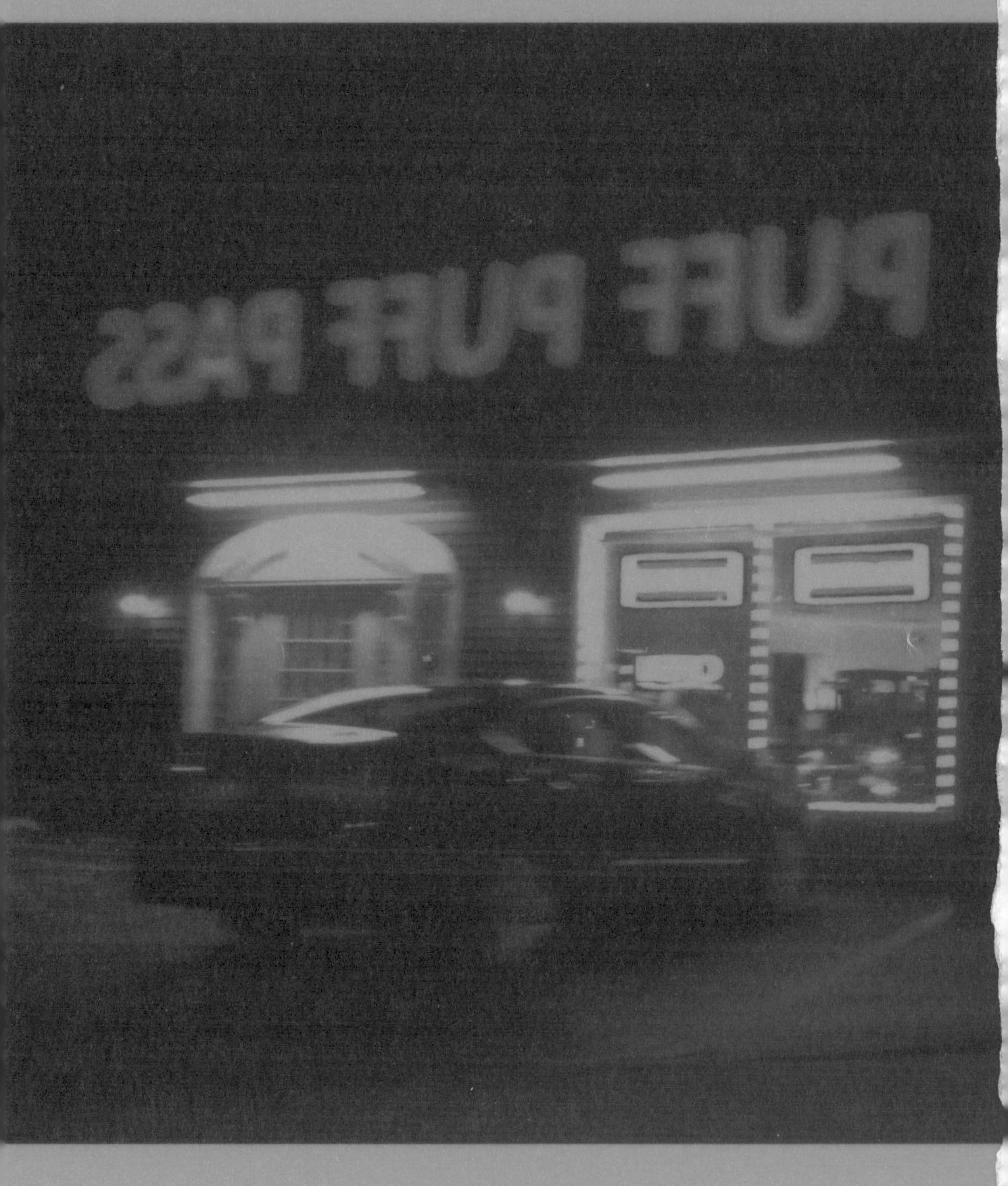
PUFF PUFF PASS

Establish a society

in which the individual

has to pay for the air he breathes

(air meters; imprisonment

and rarefied air, in

case of non-payment

simple asphyxiation if

necessary **(cut off the air)**

on condition that (?)

Ordinary brick satiates the knot.

to be tired of

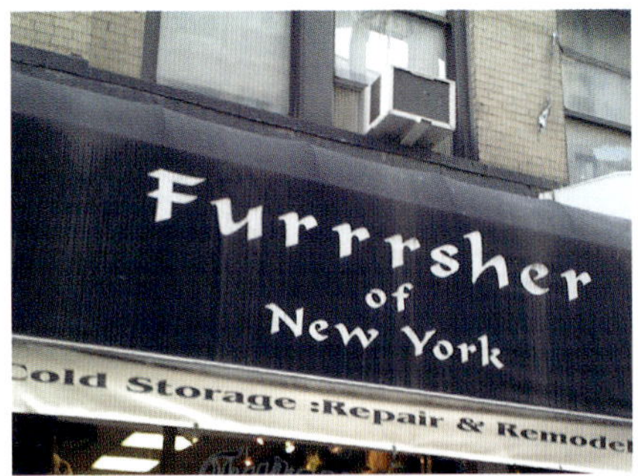
Furrrsher
of
New York
Cold Storage :Repair & Remodel

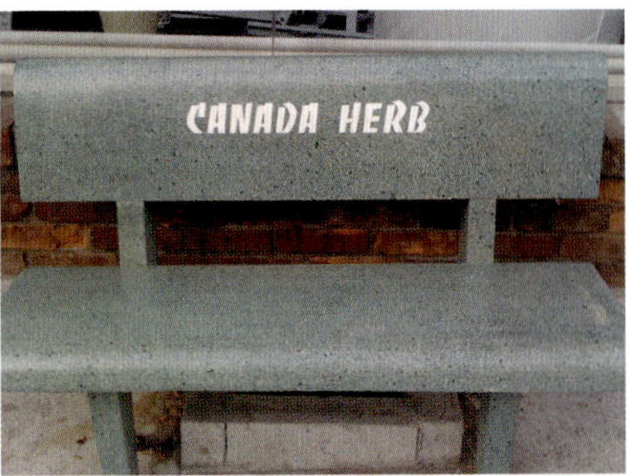
CANADA HERB

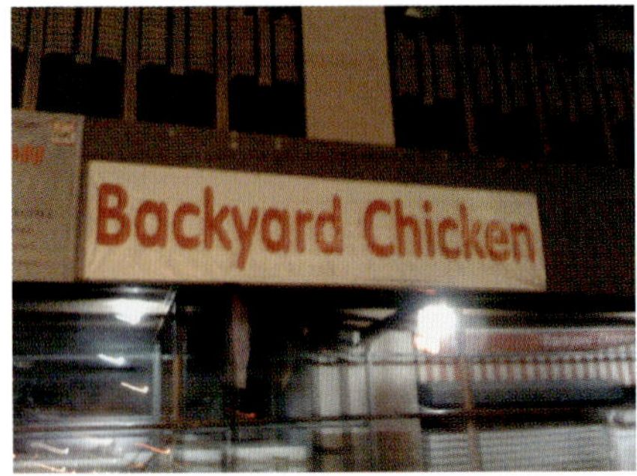
Backyard Chicken

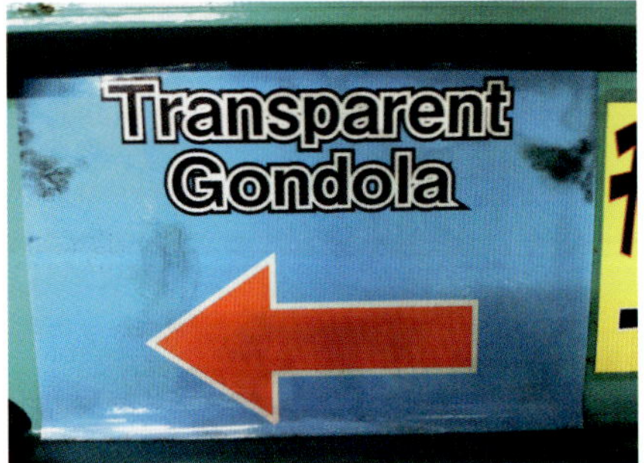
Transparent
Gondola

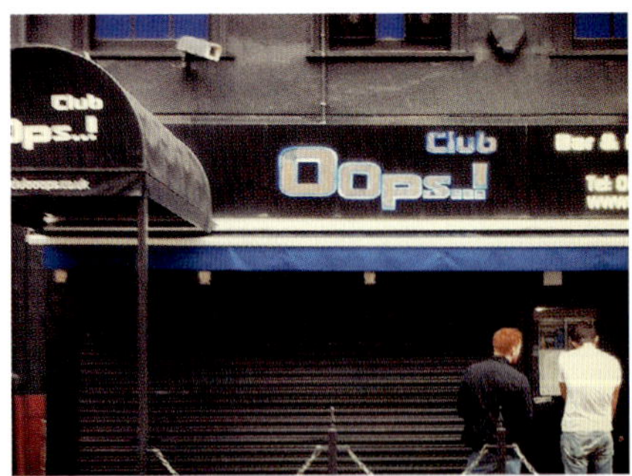
Club
Oops..!
Club
Oops..!
Bar &

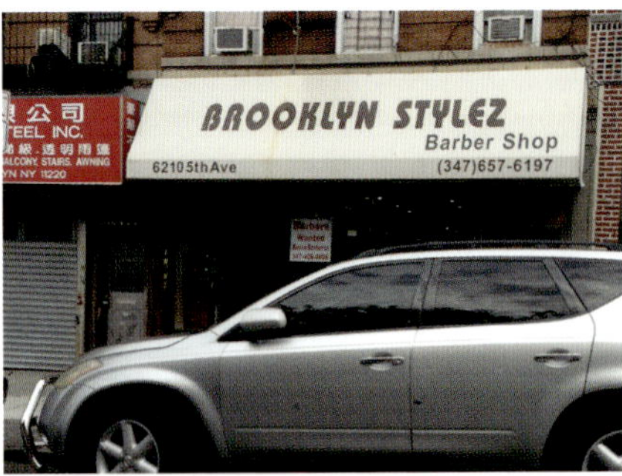
STEEL INC.
BROOKLYN STYLEZ
Barber Shop
6210 5th Ave
(347)657-6197

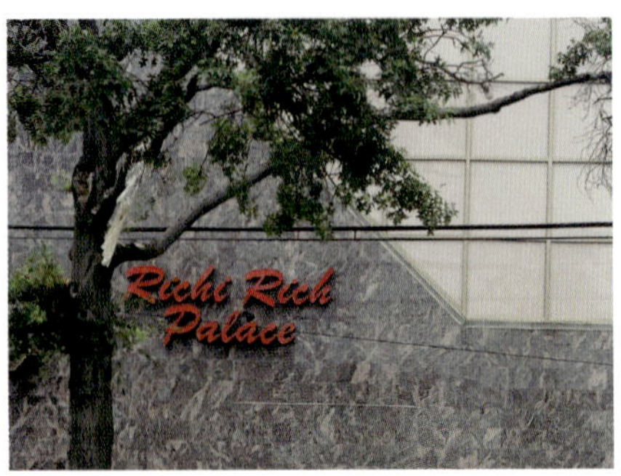
Richi Rich
Palace

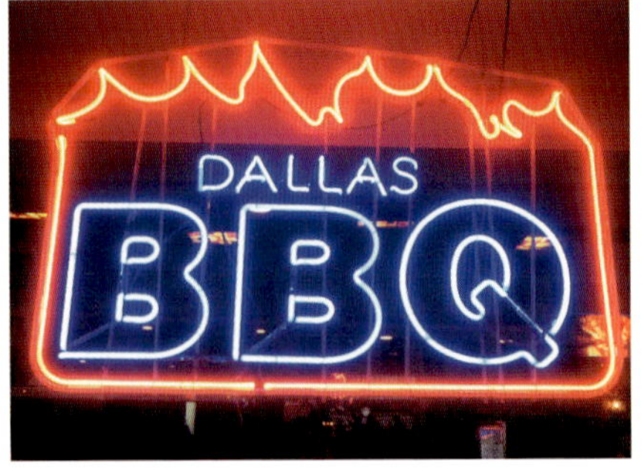
DALLAS
BBQ

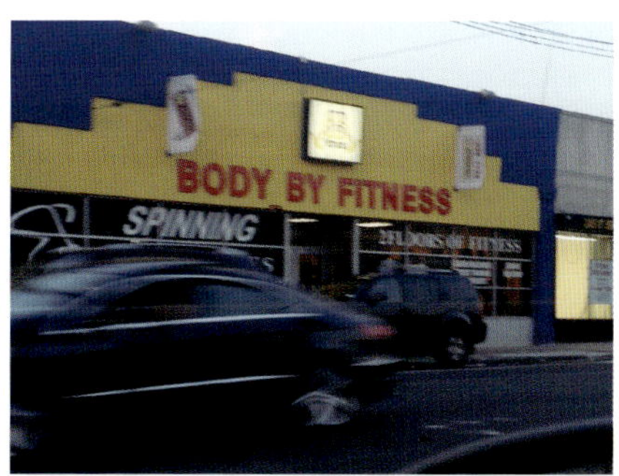
BODY BY FITNESS
SPINNING
FLOORS OF FITNESS

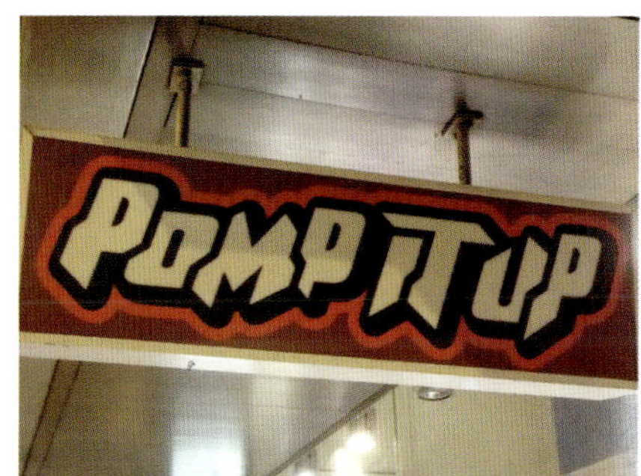
POMP IT UP

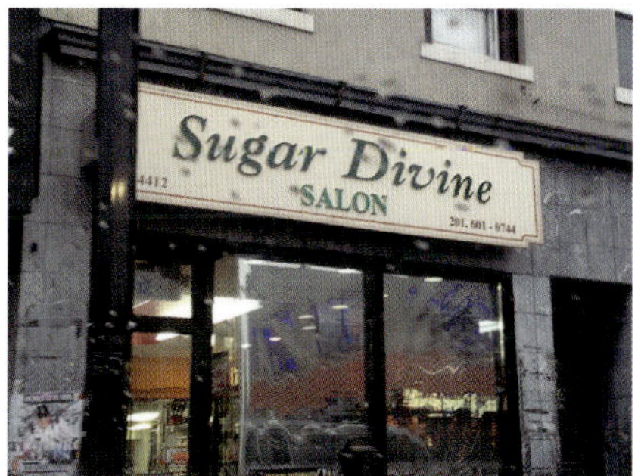
Sugar Divine
SALON
4412
201. 601 - 9744

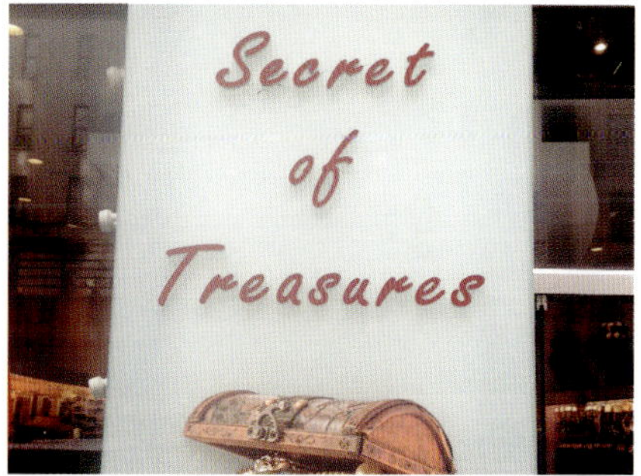
Secret
of
Treasures

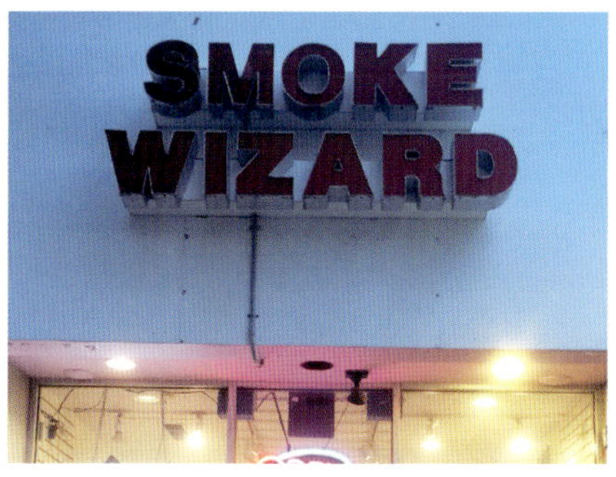
SMOKE
WIZARD

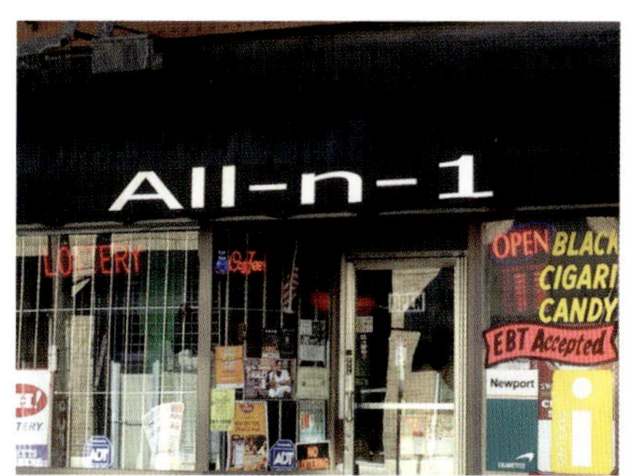
All-n-1
LOTTERY
OPEN
BLACK
CIGARI
CANDY
EBT Accepted
Newport

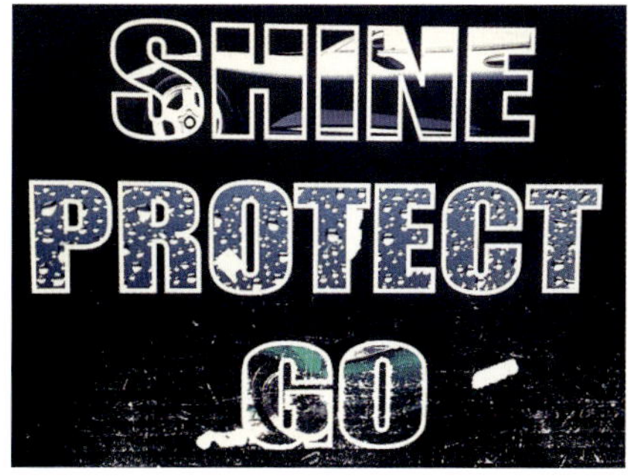
SHINE
PROTECT
GO

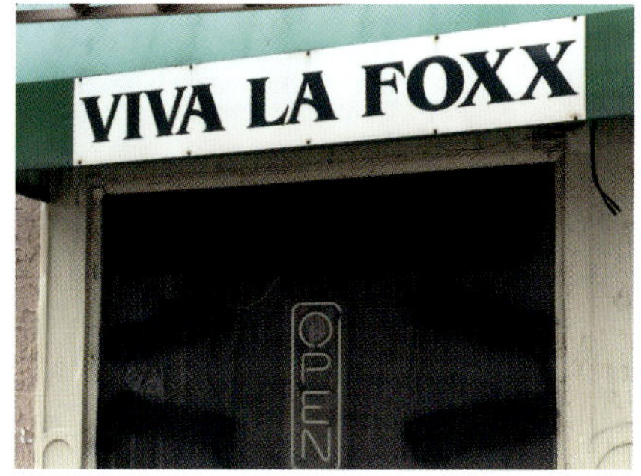
VIVA LA FOXX
OPEN

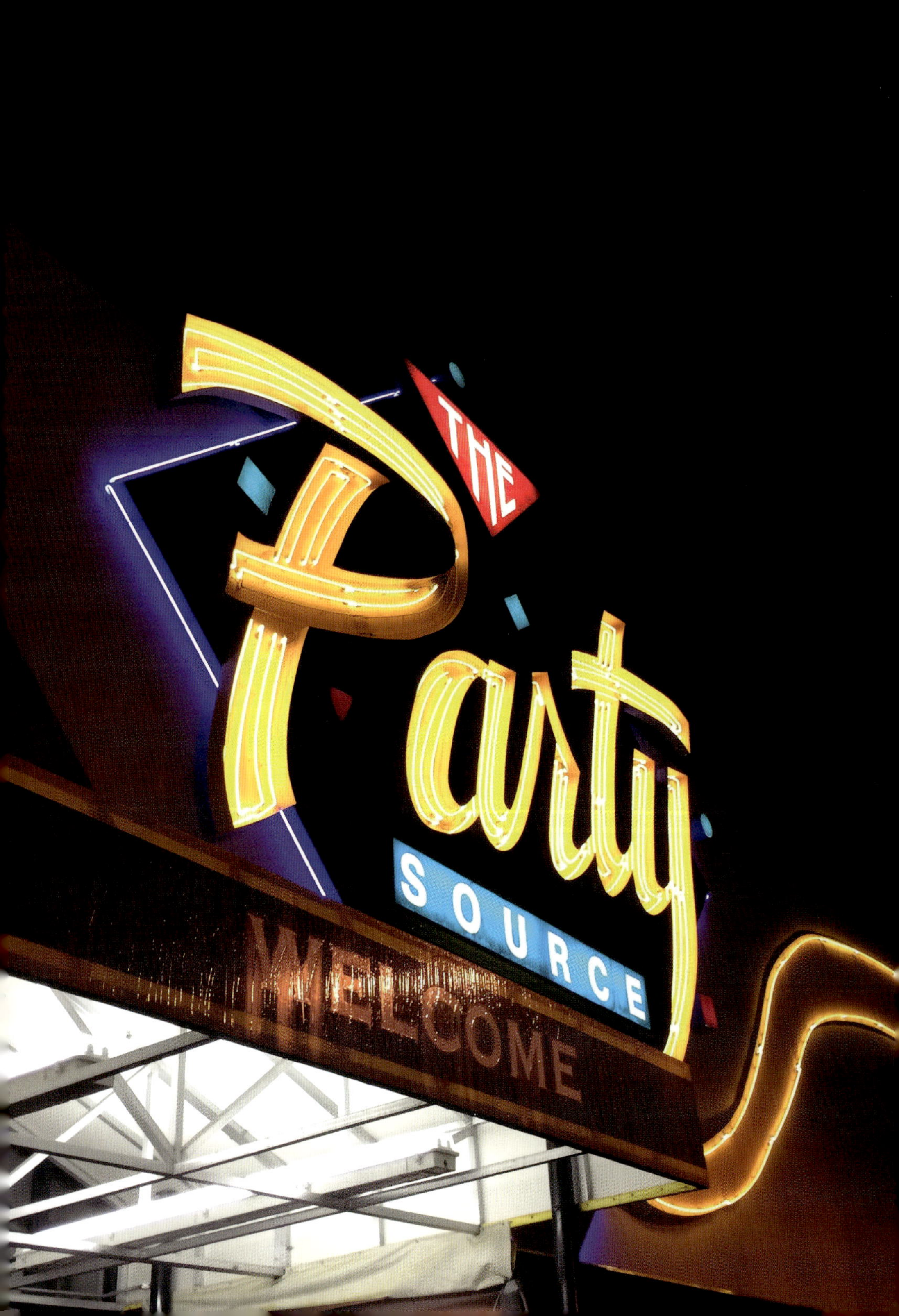

THE
Party
SOURCE
WELCOME

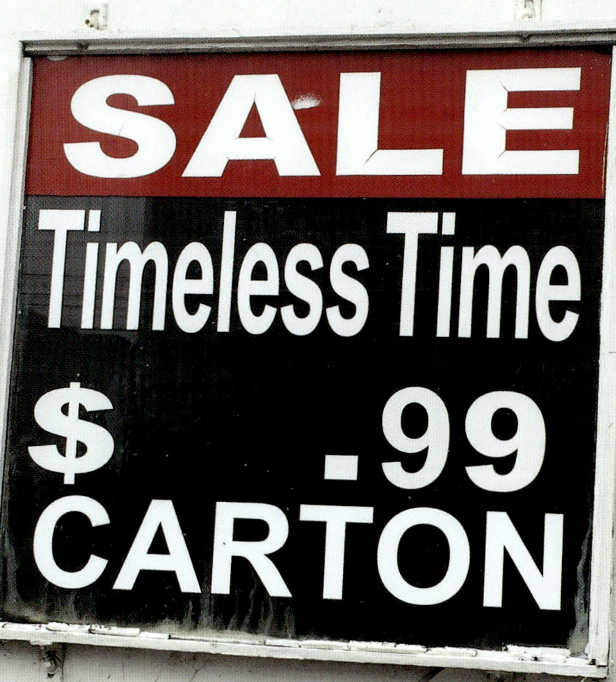
PARKING
VIOLATORS WILL BE TOWED
AT THEIR EXPENSE · K.R.S. 189·725
SALE
Timeless Time
$ .99
CARTON

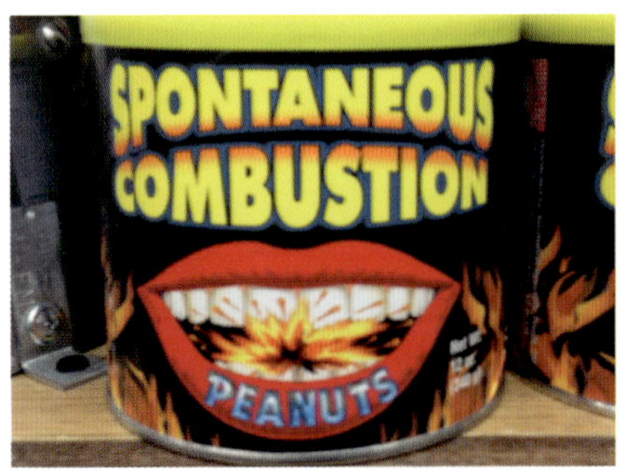

SPONTANEOUS
COMBUSTION
PEANUTS

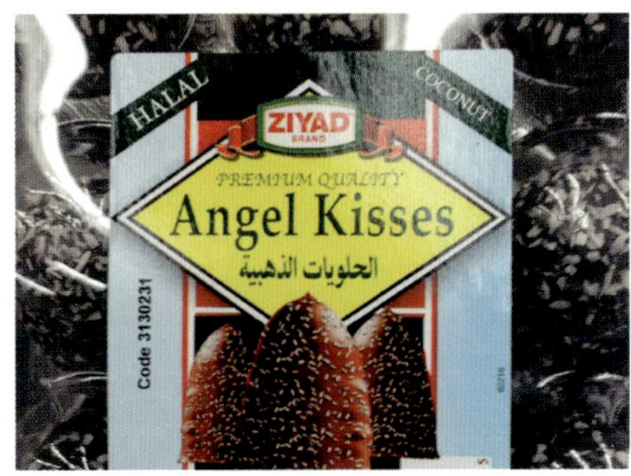

HALAL
COCONUT
ZIYAD
BRAND
PREMIUM QUALITY
Angel Kisses
الحلويات الذهبية
Code 3130231

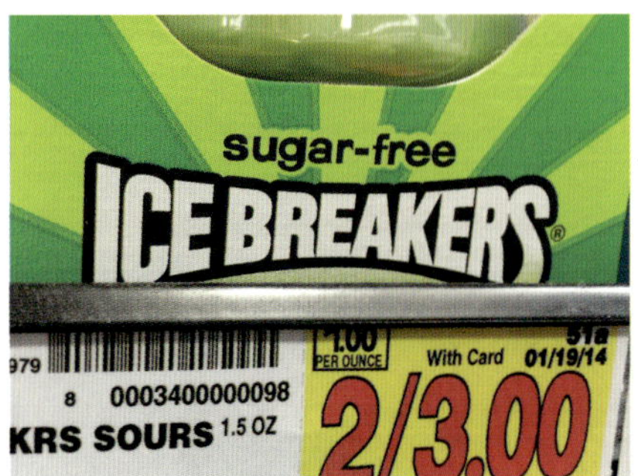

sugar-free
ICE BREAKERS
979
8   0003400000098
KRS SOURS 1.5 OZ
1.00
PER OUNCE
With Card
01/19/14
51a
2/3.00

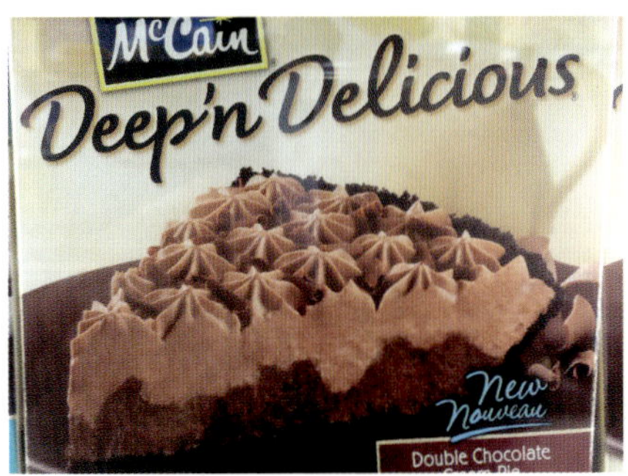

McCain
Deep'n Delicious
New
Nouveau
Double Chocolate
Cream Pie

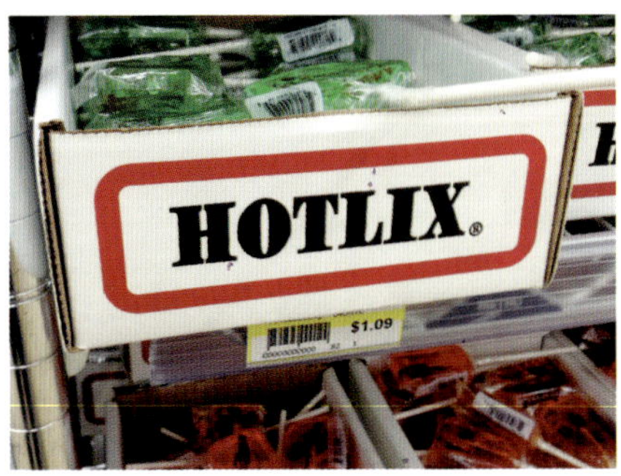

HOTLIX®
$1.09

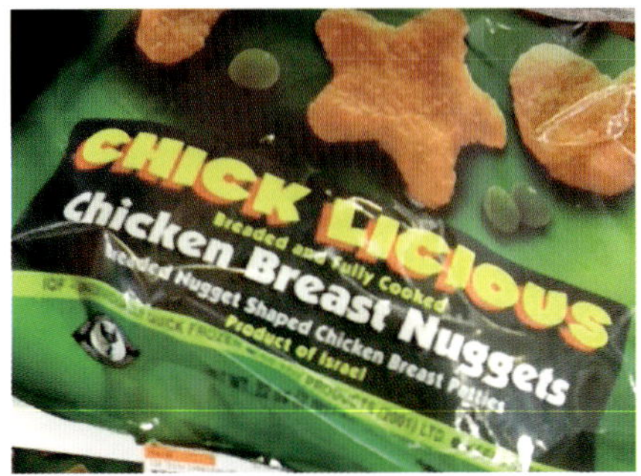

CHICK LICIOUS
Blended and Fully Cooked
Chicken Breast Nuggets
Breaded Nugget Shaped Chicken Breast Patties
QUICK FROZEN
Product of Israel

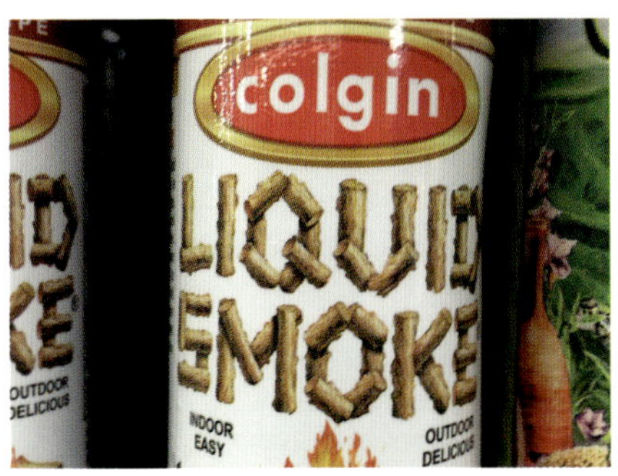

colgin
LIQUID
SMOKE
OUTDOOR
DELICIOUS
INDOOR
EASY
OUTDOOR
DELICIOUS

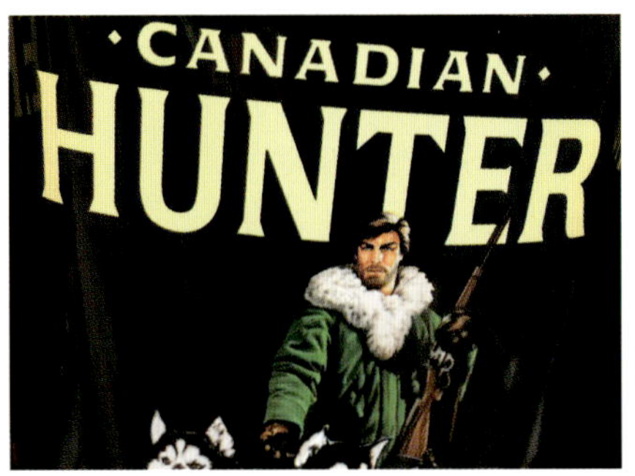

·CANADIAN·
HUNTER

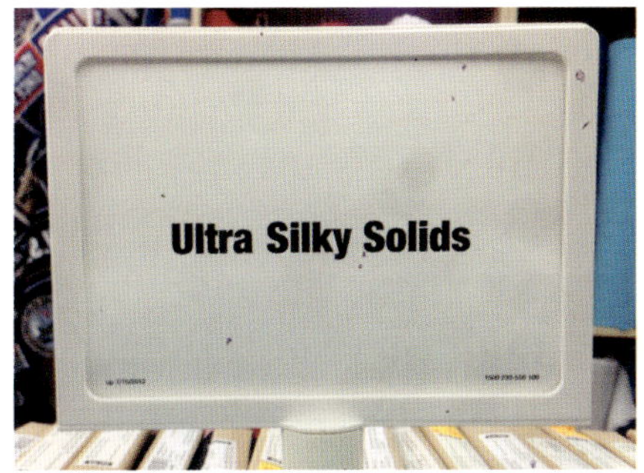
Ultra Silky Solids

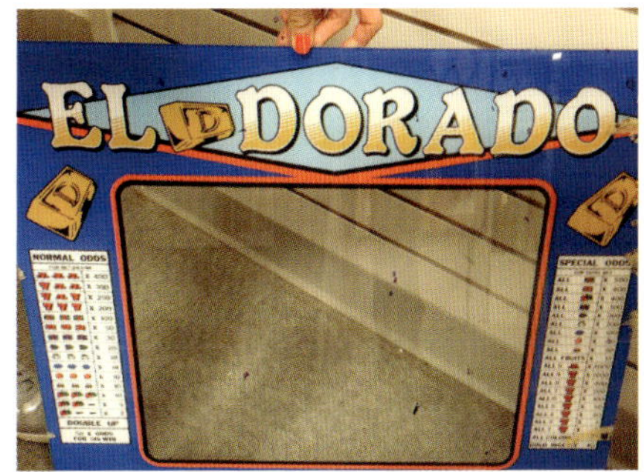
EL DORADO
NORMAL ODDS
SPECIAL ODDS
DOUBLE UP

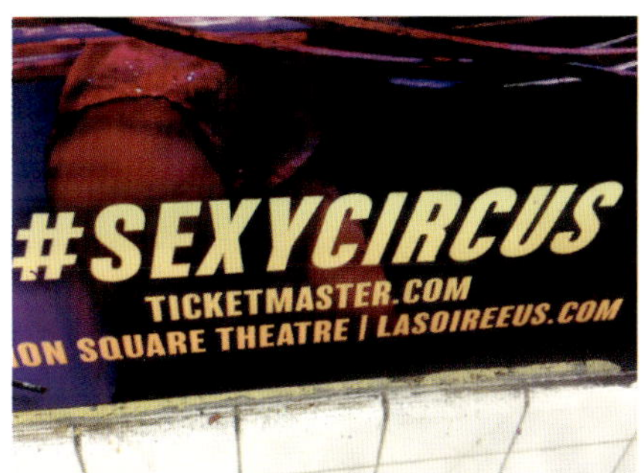
#SEXYCIRCUS
TICKETMASTER.COM
ON SQUARE THEATRE | LASOIREEUS.COM

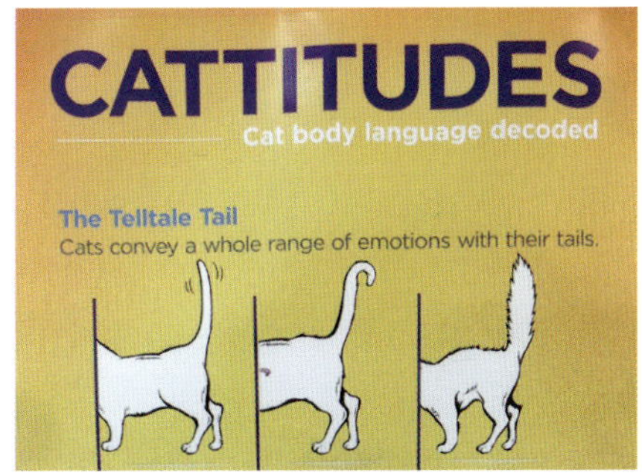
CATTITUDES
Cat body language decoded
The Telltale Tail
Cats convey a whole range of emotions with their tails.

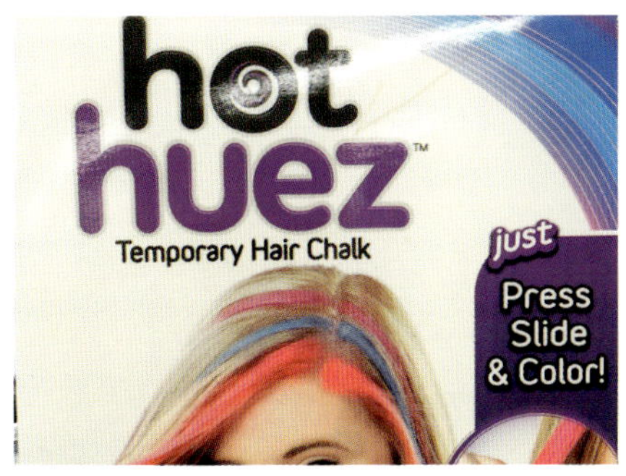
hot
huez
Temporary Hair Chalk
just
Press
Slide
& Color!

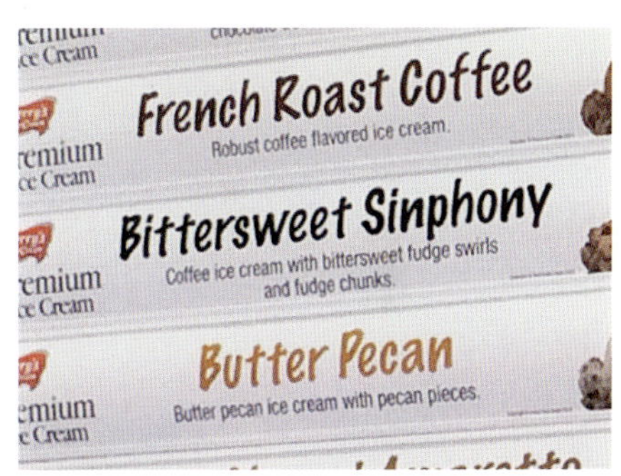
French Roast Coffee
Robust coffee flavored ice cream.
Bittersweet Sinphony
Coffee ice cream with bittersweet fudge swirls
and fudge chunks.
Butter Pecan
Butter pecan ice cream with pecan pieces.

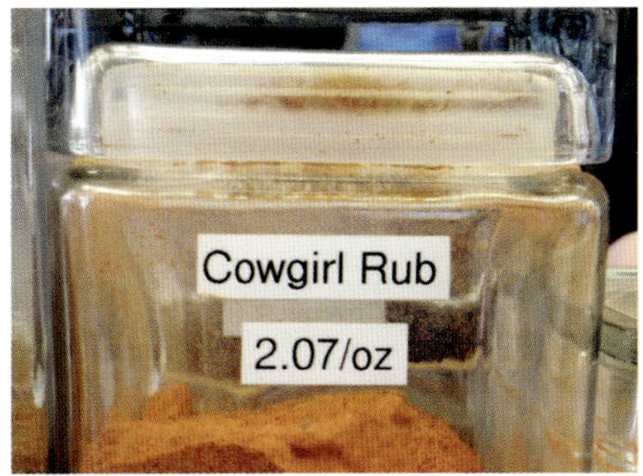
Cowgirl Rub
2.07/oz

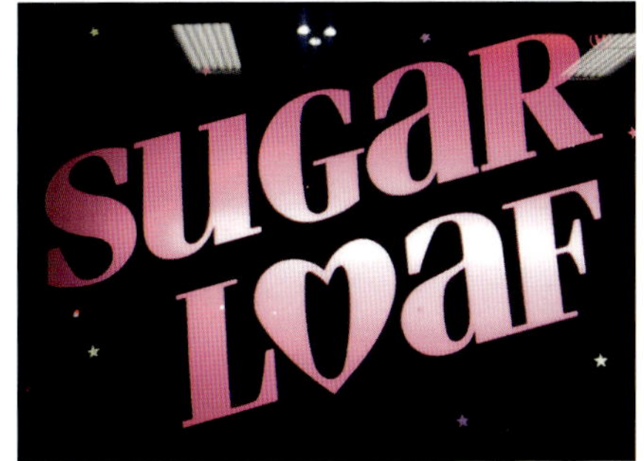
SUGAR
LOAF

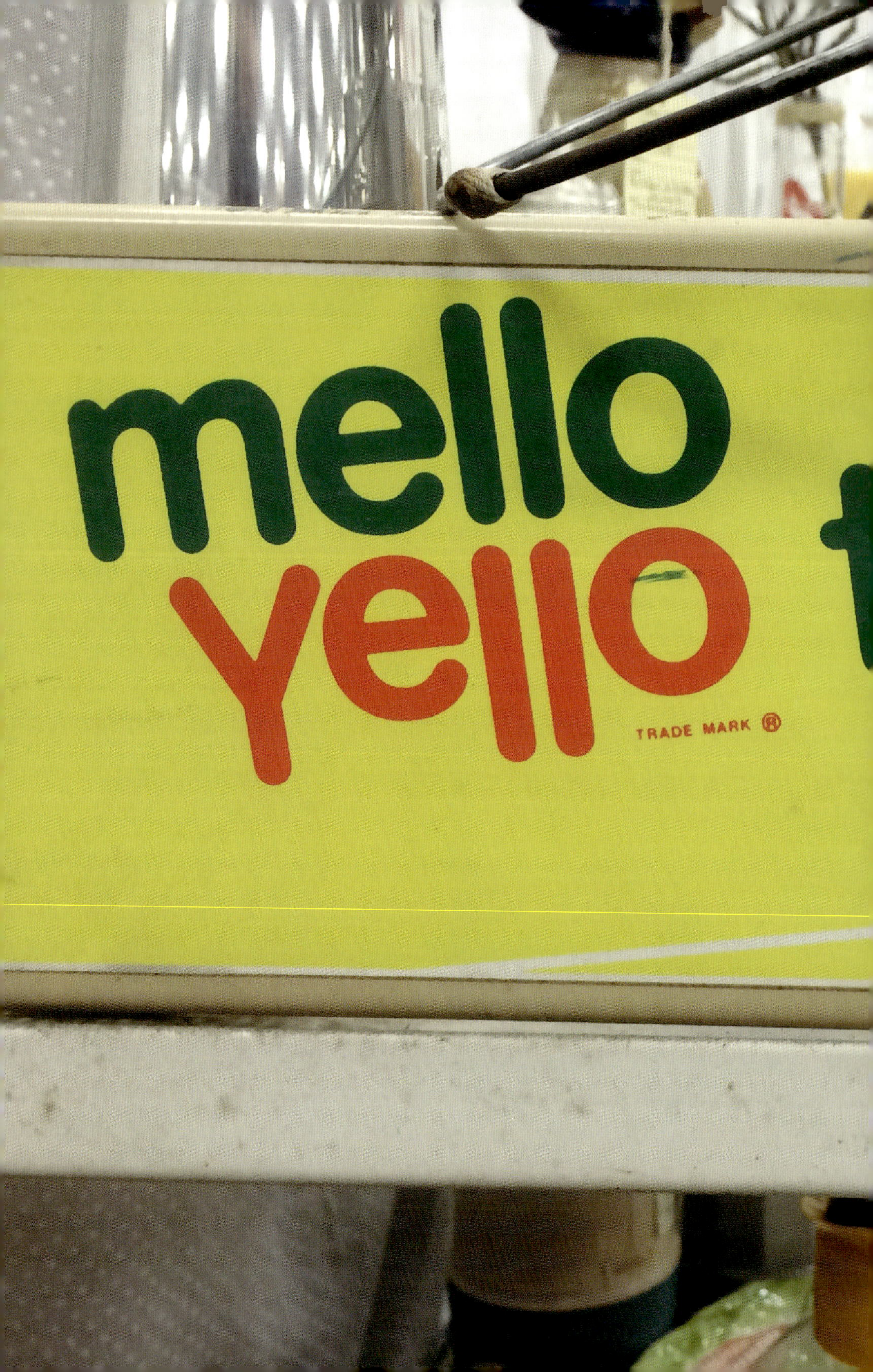

mello
yello
TRADE MARK ®

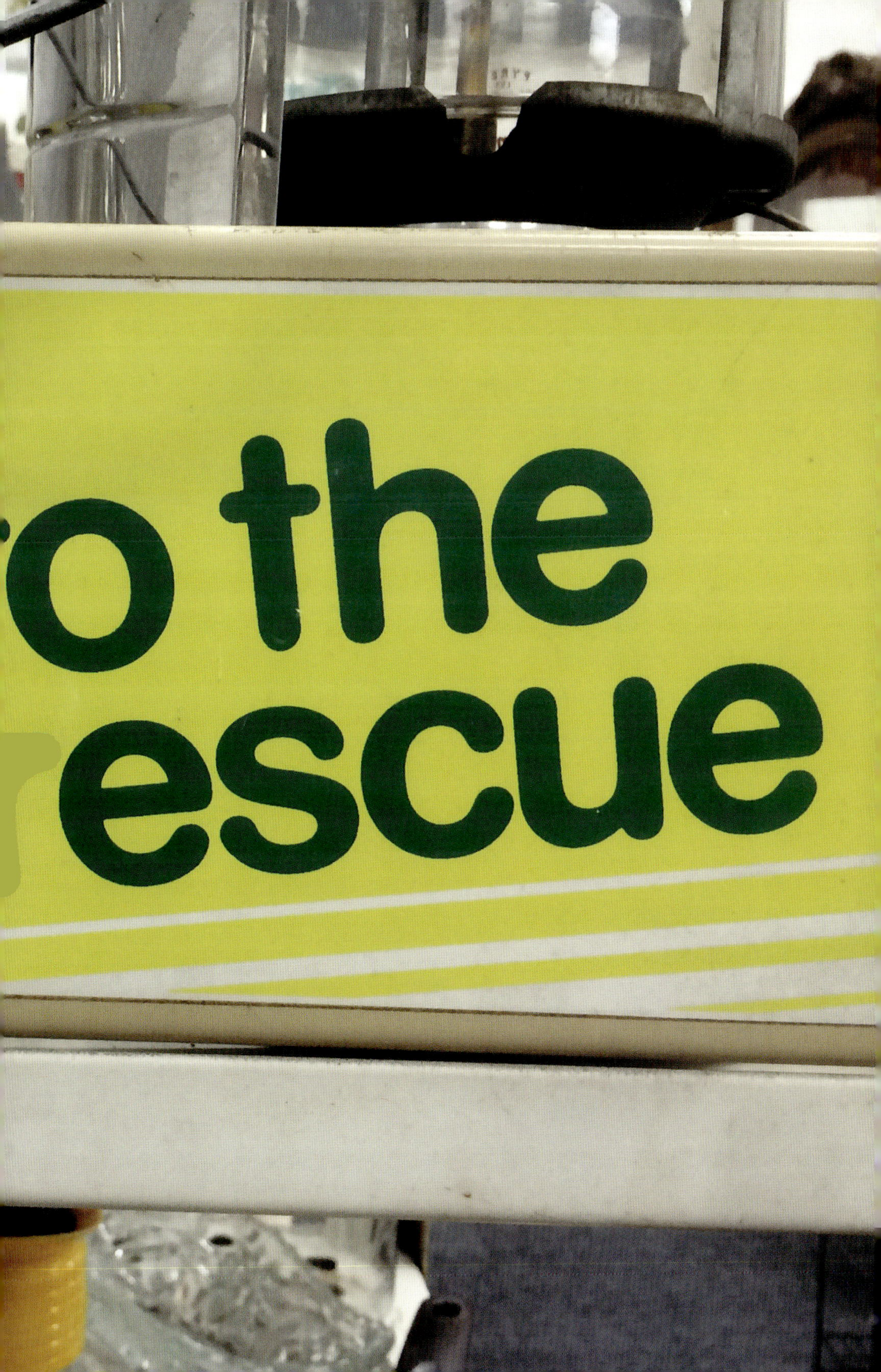
o the
escue

JULIA DAULT (b. 1977, Toronto, Canada) creates abstract paintings and sculptures that often reveal the processes of their own making. Dault sometimes uses unusual materials such as vinyl, silk, and spandex as the support of her paintings. She first builds up multiple layers of paint, and then through a process of removal, exposes the underlying composition using industrial tools such as squeegees, combs, sponges, and foam blocks. Indicative of Post-Minimalism and Conceptual art, each painting is crafted with these tools as a way to set self-imposed rules that govern the making of the work. Many of Dault's sculptures similarly fuse the industrial with the handmade. Some employ plexiglas and Formica that she bends and rolls into shape, then tenuously attaches to the wall; others are inspired by the fretworks of colorful PEX tubing plumbers install behind walls. Their abstract compositions explore—and introduce imperfections to—vernacular industrial materials, and underscore the value of engaging with the intricate and often beautiful systems that lie just beyond any given surface.

Alex Klein

At the Seams

Among my first meaningful encounters with art were the many school trips I took to the Philadelphia Museum of Art. My classmates and I were intrigued by the hidden corners of the enormous neoclassical building, filled with mysterious encounters. It felt magical to weave our way through different geographical and temporal dimensions and never exactly know how to retrace our steps. One section in particular held special appeal. After traversing a long corridor, you come upon a cluster of Van Gogh and Cézanne paintings hung around a small wishing well. Continuing through a series of smaller galleries, you arrive in an especially intriguing alcove where a bicycle is attached to a stool, a urinal is placed on its side, and a bottle rack hangs suspended. Parallel to a large window that looks out over the plaza sits a strange sculpture made of cracked glass. I now, of course, know it to be Marcel Duchamp's *The Bride Stripped Bare by Her Bachelors, Even (The Large Glass)* (1915–1923), but at the time it registered as part divider, screen, and shadow maker. It was also remarkable because it was clearly "broken."

Each time we ventured into this section of the museum, a small group of my classmates—usually boys—would disappear around a darkened corner of the gallery and reemerge with mischievous grins. Within what seems like an empty and unremarkable room with worn carpet is what appears to be an old wooden door offset by a stone border. Within the door are two small peepholes discolored from the pressure placed upon them by numerous bodies and the eyes that had peered through them. The view was beyond reach for most of us, and it wasn't until a few years later, when I was tall enough, that I was able to actually see what was on the other side. As an adult, I've intellectualized Duchamp's *Étant donnés: 1° la chute d'eau, 2° le gaz d'éclairage . . .* (1946–1966) as an entanglement of kitsch, desire, and trauma, but encountering it as a child it felt naughty, shocking, and strange. I wondered: "Was this for me? Was I supposed to see this? And the boys?"

Bound up with these memories are also the adjacent galleries. Cy Twombly's series of paintings dedicated to Homer's *Iliad* was a code to be deciphered, and in the next room, devoted to Brancusi, a special domed ceiling framed an elegant arrangement of marble, wood, and metal. Set off from this sculptural constellation was yet another closed door with an equally mysterious allure. Painted white, with a keyhole smudged around its edges from years of use, it has the air of a utility closet until you notice that it is also demarcated by a decorative stone frame. I was always intrigued by this door only to eventually discover that it is in fact the rear entrance to *Étant donnés*. Although my teachers had ignored the headless and hairless nude laying prostrate with her legs splayed open, by this time I was more familiar with Duchamp's women. "Stripped bare," I knew them to be rendered abstract through part objects, decapitation, and drag, and suggested by means of traces, impressions, and doubles. But there was also now a familiarity with the things that were kept studiously out of view—the doors that won't open, the boxes that are sealed shut, and the hinges that don't move. To understand that an object or an image is not always legible on its surface, nor is it always exactly what it seems, also opens up larger questions of historicity about what is made visible and what is occluded. As these remembrances accrued, I, too, learned to enter art and art history through other doors.

*

Art historian Richard Meyer has observed that the term "contemporary" within art history has not always signified the "new." Instead, he reminds us that "contemporary art is a relational condition."[1] That is, artworks live in a shifting state of relevance and contemporaneity. He likens them to time travelers that inhabit a "dialectical model of history in which the past is no more settled or secure than the present," and in which their function shifts between that of "emissary," "historical relic," and "interlocutor."[2] This model has the potential to chafe against a linear and teleological approach to time and history forged under false notions of progress, and ultimately in the service of hegemonic (and heteronormative) powers. Similarly, curator Lynne Cooke has asked us to be wary of recuperative gestures that do not, in turn, undermine the foundations upon which structural inequities were forged in the first place, instead proposing a methodology of "reconciliation;" Julia Bryan-Wilson has championed the art historian's engagement with the "fray;" and the late architecture

---

1 Richard Meyer, *What Was Contemporary Art?* (Cambridge: MIT Press, 2013), p.16.
2 Ibid, pp.24-34.

critic Detlef Mertins has proposed an understanding of modernity and modernism that is "unbound."[3] Such models also extend to artists who, by way of plastic and conceptual formations, forge dialogues with unforeclosed projects of the past within the present.

To revisit the forms of previous moments might also be a way to reposition the people and the strategies that produced them. If the "what if?" of history is played on a recursive loop, for artists there is the chance to enact alternatives, not just of how we understand the past, but how we articulate the organization of the future. While such operations offer a chance to reignite the prospects of failed utopias and revolutions, they also place value on different ways of being, thinking, and relating, necessarily troubling the parameters of who is implicitly included in the category of "we."

To be sure, western modernism has often been a marriage of the irreconcilable, of opposing orders and influences stitched together in the service of a particular vision of the avant-garde. There are forms that have masqueraded as "other" subjectivities and abstractions that have colonized "other" cultures, time periods, and positionalities, all in the service of the modern, or what we might understand today to be the contemporary. Here, we could point to examples such as the pervasive modernist fetishization of what was once categorized as "primitive," to the Albers's fascination with the ancient architecture of Latin America, or even to Alfred Barr's presentation of cave paintings in the Museum of Modern Art. With historical distance, the problematics of these inquiries are made increasingly legible, as are the untidy socio-political conditions that initially produced them. And while we might now take issue with some of these methodologies, as well as the predominantly white male perspectives they represent, we must also appreciate the drives that initially produced them. For these artists, too, were looking for different ways to proceed under the threat of fascism. Indeed, these works were often made in the face of persecution, fashioning what T. J. Demos, writing on Duchamp, has argued is an art history of exile.

<hr>

3 See Lynne Cooke, *Outliers and American Vanguard Art*, (Chicago: University of Chicago Press, 2018), p.24; Julia Bryan-Wilson, *Fray: Art and Textile Politics*, (Chicago: University of Chicago Press, 2017); and Detlef Mertins, *Modernity Unbound: Other Histories of Architectural Modernity*, (London: Architectural Association Publications, 2011).

For example, Duchamp's *Boîte-en-valise* (1935–1941) can be read as both a comment on the authenticity of the art object in the face of mechanical reproduction and as a packed suitcase ready to go at a moment's notice.[4]

Yet, even as we attempt these sorts of re-narrativizations, we must necessarily acknowledge the projects that never happened in the first place. How many individuals were excluded by the parameters that undergird the authority of the museum and the art historian by means of qualifiers such as "skill," "quality," and "taste;" categories such as the "decorative," "craft," or "self-taught;" or intended pejoratives such as the "domestic," "personal," or "emotional?" To note just one of many possible examples, Walter Gropius, the founder of the Bauhaus, believed that women thought in two-dimensions and that men thought in three. As a result, female students were directed towards weaving and male students were encouraged to pursue architecture. While this undoubtedly lead to a hierarchization of the Bauhaus students' output, it also precluded the possibility of the development of another form of modernism.

*

A "vanishing mediator" is a term employed in literary theory to describe something that enables the transition from one movement or periodization to another. While acting as a crucial catalyst for change, it disappears in the process. In psychoanalytic theory the vanishing mediator has also been linked to the gendered category of hysteria, serving as a physical marker of the manifestation of a crisis while simultaneously mediating its eventual resolution. Within the domain of art, we might extend this term to describe the many individuals who have mediated between seemingly discrete positions and periodicities, only to find their contributions made invisible. Or, to use a more material metaphor, such figures could be said to function as a kind of hinge or seam. Even as they attempt to render whole what is separate, they also mark a site of suturing, stitching, or joining. In revisiting the historical moments of modernism, artists working today can look to these figures and fissures

4 See T.J. Demos, *The Exiles of Marcel Duchamp*, (Cambridge: MIT Press, 2007).

as opportunities for disclosure and revelation and as an antidote to the pervasive amnesia—both in art history and in art's spaces of display—with regard to modernism's many returns and misreadings. But to do so is not a call to erase the problems embedded in these forms, but to ask how one might begin to unravel their complications, or even to begin to dismantle the project of modernism at its seams.